Editor
Lorin Klistoff, M.A.

Illustrator
Vicki Frazier

Cover Artist
Brenda DiAntonis

Managing Editor
Karen J. Goldfluss, M.S. Ed.

Creative Director
Karen J. Goldfluss, M.S. Ed.

Art Production Manager
Kevin Barnes

Art Coordinator
Renée Christine Yates

Imaging
Denise Thomas
Nathan Rivera

Publisher
Mary D. Smith, M.S. Ed.

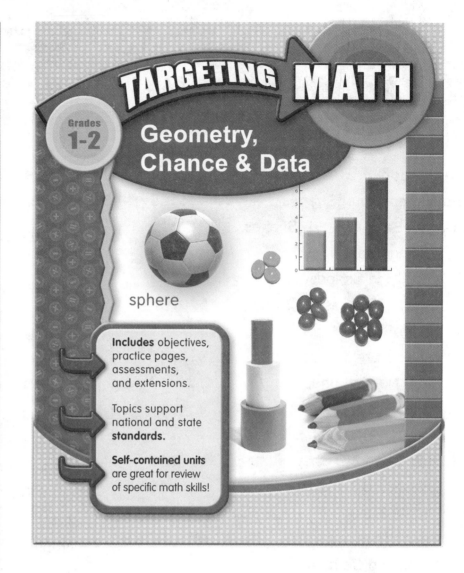

Authors

Nicole Bauer, Judy Tertini, and Helen Carmody

(Revised and rewritten by Teacher Created Resources, Inc.)

Teacher Created Resources, Inc.
6421 Industry Way
Westminster, CA 92683
www.teachercreated.c

ISBN-13: 978-1-4206-

© 2007 Teacher Created Re

Made in U.S.A.

The classroom teacher may reproduce copies of materials in this book for classroom use only. Reproduction of any part for an entire school or school system is strictly prohibited. No part of this publication may be transmitted, stored, or recorded in any form without written permission from the publisher.

Table of Contents

Table of Contents

Introduction

Targeting Math

The series *Targeting Math* is a comprehensive classroom resource. It has been developed so that teachers can find activities and reproducible pages for all areas of the math curriculum.

About This Series

The twelve books in the series cover all aspects of the math curriculum in an easy-to-access format. Each of the three levels has four books: Numeration and Fractions; Operations and Number Patterns; Geometry, Chance and Data; and Measurement. Each topic in a book is covered by one or more units that are progressive in level. The teacher is able to find resources for all students whatever their ability. This enables the teacher to differentiate for different ability groups. It also provides an easy way to find worksheets at different levels for remediation and extension.

About This Book

Targeting Math: Geometry, Chance and Data (Grades 1 and 2) contains the following topics: two-dimensional shapes, three-dimensional shapes, position and mapping/transformation, graphs, and chance and data. There are also a few additional resources at the end of the book (pages 105–110). These pages can be cut out and used for manipulatives or for shape identification. Each topic is covered by two complete units of work. (See Table of Contents for specific skills.)

About Each Unit

Each unit is complete in itself. It begins with a list of objectives, resources needed, mathematical language used, and a description of each student activity page. This is followed by suggested student activities to reinforce learning. The reproducible pages cover different aspects of the topic in a progressive nature and all answers are included. Every unit includes an assessment page. These assessment pages are important resources in themselves as teachers can use them to find out what their students know about a new topic. They can also be used for assessing specific outcomes when clear feedback is needed.

About the Skills Index

A Skills Index is provided at the end of the book. It lists objectives for the student pages of each unit in the book.

#8991 Targeting Math: Geometry, Chance and Data   © *Teacher Created Resources, Inc.*

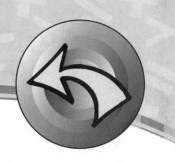

TWO-DIMENSIONAL SHAPES

These units provide opportunities to identify, name, classify, and draw two-dimensional shapes. Students identify regular shapes, trace shapes, and order shapes according to size. Similarities and differences are recognized, and shapes are created by joining dots. Corners and sides are counted. Lines are explored and patterns made by drawing lines. The activity page involves moving counters on a grid to meet specific requirements. There is one assessment page at the end of each unit.

5

BEGINNING 2-D SHAPES

Unit 1

Sort
Classify
Identify
Name
Order

Objectives

- sorts and describes objects in terms of their features, such as size and shape
- recognizes, names, and makes simple two-dimensional shapes and describes their properties using everyday language by observing similarities and differences
- interprets and begins to use terms relating to shape to distinguish similarities and differences
- generally recognizes and names triangles, rectangles, circles and common simple shapes
- names mathematical shapes that can be found as components of familiar things

Language

shape(s), rectangle, square, circle, triangle, same shape, oval, different, order, size, smallest, largest, curved

Materials/Resources

colored pencils, scissors, glue

Contents of Student Pages

- * Materials needed for each reproducible student page

Page 8 Sorting Shapes
sorting circles, triangles, and squares
- * blue, red, and green pencils

Page 9 Identifying Shapes
Identifying circles, squares, triangles, and rectangles
- * red, yellow, blue, and green pencils

Page 10 Drawing Shapes
tracing two-dimensional shapes and labeling; copying two-dimensional shapes

Page 11 Same Shapes
Identifying similarities and differences of two-dimensional shapes; making their own design using shapes
- * colored pencils

Page 12 Naming Shapes
naming two-dimensional shapes; matching shapes to their names

Page 13 More Naming Shapes
Identifying and ordering two-dimensional shapes

Page 14 Assessment
- * colored pencils

Page 15 Activity—Blast Off
- * colored pencils, scissors, glue

. . . .
Remember

Before starting ensure each student:
❑ has a sharp pencil.

© Teacher Created Resources, Inc.

Additional Activities

- ❏ Give the students opportunities to play with puzzles, boxes, and construction toys to develop an awareness of shape.
- ❏ Eat differently-shaped foods (e.g., star biscuits, circular crackers). Have a shape party.
- ❏ Allow the students to play with dough. Give them cookie cutters in different shapes so they can explore.
- ❏ Give students differently-shaped paper to paint on.
- ❏ Make shape Bingo cards for the students to practice shape recognition.
- ❏ Cut shapes (e.g., circles) out of cardboard in different sizes and encourage students to order the size.
- ❏ Obtain a collection of lids and use them in a variety of ways. Students can draw around them or make a master board showing outlines of the lids. Students can match lids with outlines.
- ❏ Provide students with a variety of craft activities so they can experiment with shapes (e.g., splattering, printing, collage).
- ❏ Give the students weaving mats in different shapes.
- ❏ Give the students a variety of shapes to sort.
- ❏ Have a board of shapes. Choose one shape at a time and encourage students to cut shapes out of magazines or catalogs.
- ❏ Go out of the classroom, and if possible, into the community for a "shape walk." Record the findings.
- ❏ Make class or individual shape books.
- ❏ Read books to the students, such as Spot Looks at Shapes by Eric Hill or Shapes by Jan Pienkowski.

Answers

Page 8 Sorting Shapes
Make sure circles are blue, squares are red, and triangles are green. Also, make sure each shape has a line drawn to its correct box.

Page 9 Identifying Shapes
Make sure all circles are red, squares are yellow, triangles are blue, and rectangles are green.

Page 10 Drawing Shapes
1. Make sure shapes are traced.
   a. rectangle
   b. square
   c. circle
   d. triangle
2. Make sure all shapes are copied correctly.

Page 11 Same Shapes
1. a. The first, third, and fourth shirts from the left of the line should be colored.
   b. The second and fourth shirts from the left of the line should be colored.
   c. The second, third, and fourth shirts from the left of the line should be colored.
   d. The first and third shirts from the left of the line should be colored.
2. Make sure each shirt is designed with the designated shape.

Page 12 Naming Shapes
1. a. oval
   b. circle
   c. rectangle
   d. square
2. Make sure that each shape has a line drawn to its correct name.

Page 13 More Naming Shapes
1. a. oval
   b. circle
   c. rectangle
   d. circle
   e. oval
   f. rectangle
   g. square
   h. hexagon
2. a. 4, 2, 3, 1
   b. 1, 3, 2, 4

Page 14 Assessment
1. a. the rectangle
   b. the square
   c. the square
   d. the circle
2. 4, 1, 3, 2
3. Make sure circles are colored.
4. Make sure all shapes are traced. Make sure the curved shapes are red.
5. Make sure shapes are traced. Make sure shapes are joined to their correct names.

Page 15 Activity—Blast Off
1. 2
2. 3
3. 1
4. 1

Name	**Date**

The dog tipped the shapes out. Color the circles blue, the squares red, and the triangles green. Then, draw lines from the shapes to the correct boxes.

Name   **Date**

Color the picture.

Color circles red.

Color squares yellow.

Color triangles blue.

Color rectangles green.

© *Teacher Created Resources, Inc.*   *#8991 Targeting Math: Geometry, Chance and Data*

Name    **Date**

1. Trace the shapes and write their names.

a.

b.

rectangle
triangle
square
circle

_____

_____

c.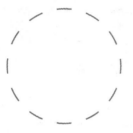

d.

_____

_____

2. Draw more of each shape.

a.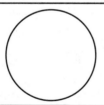

_____

b.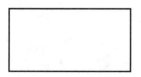

_____

c.

_____

d.

(10)

Name	**Date**

1. Color the T-shirts that have the same shapes as the first T-shirt.

2. Design your own T-shirts, using the shape under each shirt.

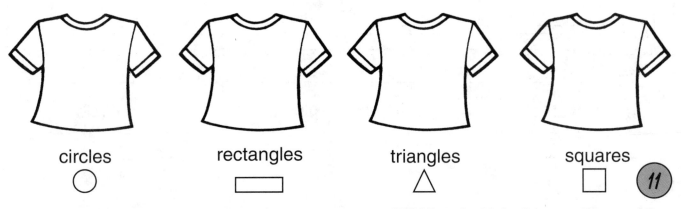

circles   rectangles   triangles   squares

11

Name   **Date**

1. Write the correct name under each shape.

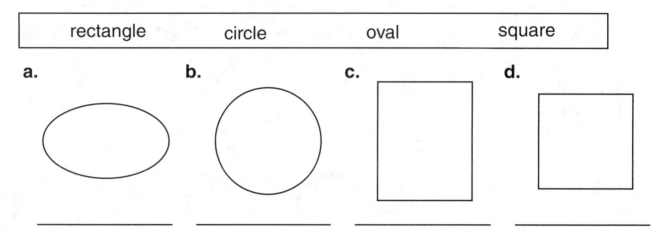

| rectangle | circle | oval | square |

a.   **b.**   **c.**   **d.**

_____   _____   _____   _____

2. Photo frames come in different shapes. Draw a line from each shape to its name.

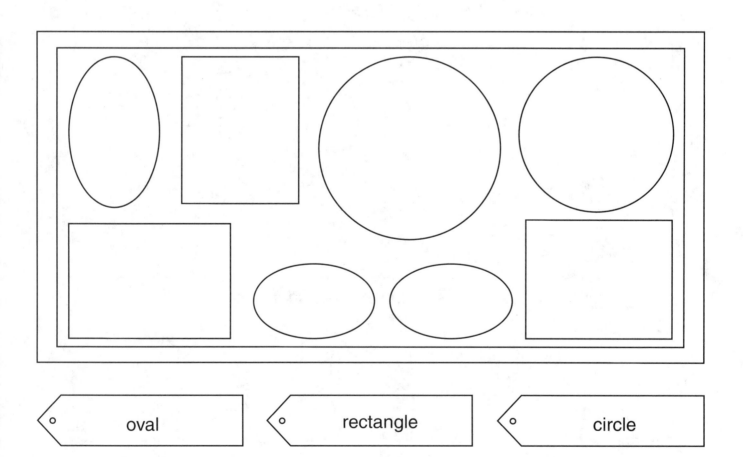

oval   rectangle   circle

#8991 Targeting Math: Geometry, Chance and Data

© *Teacher Created Resources, Inc.*

Name	**Date**

1. Objects come in different shapes. Name each shape.

| circle |
| oval |
| rectangle |
| square |
| hexagon |

a.

mat

_____

b.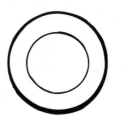

plate

_____

c.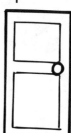

door

_____

d. clock

_____

e. belt loop

_____

f.

book

_____

g. 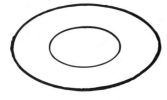 cushion

_____

h.  stop sign

_____

2. Number the objects 1 to 4 in order of size from smallest to largest.

a.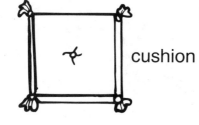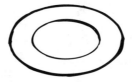

____   ____   ____   ____

b.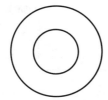

____   ____   ____   ____

© *Teacher Created Resources, Inc.*

Name	**Date**

1. Circle the shape in each row that does not belong.

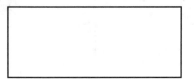 

2. Number the rectangles 1 to 4 in order of size from the smallest to the largest.

3. Color the circles.

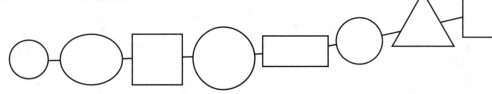

4. Trace over the shapes. Color the curved shapes red.

5. Trace the shapes and join them to their names.

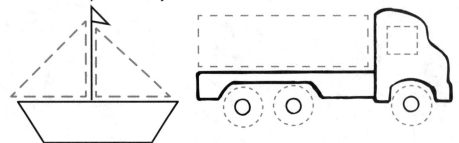

circle

triangle

rectangle

square

#8991 Targeting Math: Geometry, Chance and Data   © *Teacher Created Resources, Inc.*

Name	**Date**

Directions: Color and cut out the shapes at the bottom of the page. Glue the shapes in place to create a space ship like the one shown. Then, answer the questions.

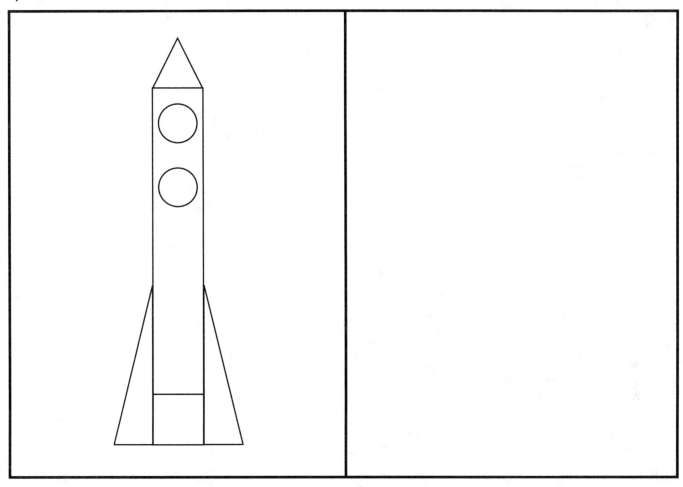

1. How many circles? _____   3. How many rectangles? _____

2. How many triangles? _____   4. How many squares? _____

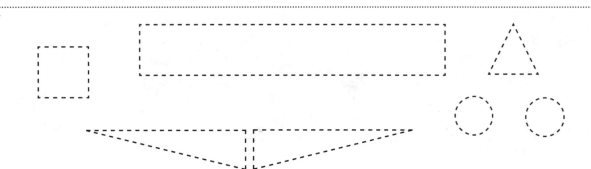

15

MORE 2-D SHAPES

Unit 2

Investigate properties
Create shapes
Complete matrix
Lines
Patterns

Objectives

- makes two-dimensional shapes using geo-boards
- makes, classifies, and names two-dimensional shapes and describes their properties
- generally recognizes and names triangles, rectangles, circles, and other common simple shapes
- matches congruent figures and objects one to one
- recognizes, describes, and makes and continues simple number and spatial patterns
- talks about likenesses and differences between things seen or handled and begins to connect shape to function
- recognizes, names, and makes simple two-dimensional shapes and describes their properties using everyday language by observing similarities and differences
- makes constructions from verbal and visual instructions

Language

geo-board, shapes, sides, how many, pattern, hexagon, circle, triangle, oblong, diamond, oval, lines, sloping, straight, broken, zigzag, wavy

Materials/Resources

geo-boards, rubber bands, colored pencils

Contents of Student Pages

* Materials needed for each reproducible student page

Page 18 Investigate 2-D Shapes
using geo-boards and counting sides of shapes

* geo-boards

Page 19 Create Shapes
creating shapes by joining dots and matching 2-D shapes

* colored pencils

Page 20 Shape Patterns
completing patterns and filling in a pattern chart

* colored pencils

Page 21 Sides and Corners
recognizing similarities and differences; counting sides and corners

* colored pencils

Page 22 Investigate Lines
identify, draw, and describe lines

* colored pencils

Page 23 Lines and Patterns
drawing line patterns, naming and drawing complex shapes

Page 24 Assessment

Remember

Before starting, ensure that each student:
- ☐ has some knowledge of two-dimensional shapes.
- ☐ knows how to use a geo-board.
- ☐ knows how to complete a matrix.

© Teacher Created Resources, Inc.

Additional Activities

- ❏ In P.E., direct students to move in different ways (e.g., walk straight, walk in a zigzag fashion).
- ❏ Use masking tape to make shapes in the playground. Direct students to move in and around the shapes.
- ❏ Provide students with a variety of craft activities so they can experiment with different lines (e.g., string painting, collage with curved, straight and zigzag pieces of paper, roller painting, candle painting).
- ❏ Give the students opportunities to make shapes with geo-boards.
- ❏ Divide the class into groups. Give each group an area in which to find shapes (e.g., kitchen, bathroom, car). Each of the groups discusses their findings and reports back to the class.
- ❏ Give students shape templates to draw around, and let them make patterns.
- ❏ Give students shape templates and encourage them to make pictures out of shapes.
- ❏ Give the students opportunities to play with shapes and to investigate properties, such as number of sides and number of corners.

Answers

Page 18 Investigate 2-D Shapes

1. Make sure shapes have four sides.
2. a. 5　　　　d. 4
   b. 3　　　　e. 6
   c. 6　　　　f. 4
3. a. Check shapes on geo-board
   b. Make sure the number of sides matches the shape.

Page 19 Create Shapes

1. a. rectangle
   b. square
   c. triangle
   d. hexagon
   e. diamond
2. Make sure shapes with the same color match.

Page 20 Shape Patterns

1. a. A circle should be drawn.
   b. A diamond should be drawn.
   c. A triangle should be drawn.
   d. A circle, square, triangle, and a square should be drawn.

2.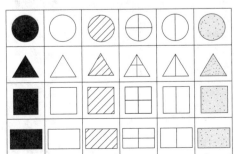

Page 21 Sides and Corners

1. a. rectangle, 4, 4
   b. hexagon, 6, 6
   c. triangle, 3, 3
   d. circle, 1, 0
2. triangle = red, square = blue, hexagon = yellow, rectangle = blue, diamond = blue
3. a. triangle
   b. octagon
   c. second shape
   d. hexagon

Page 22 Investigate Lines

1. a. zigzag
   b. wavy
   c. straight
   d. broken
   e. sloping
2. a. Design should include zigzag lines.
   b. Design should include sloping lines.
   c. Design should include wavy lines.
3. Teacher to check.

Page 23 Lines and Patterns

1. Teacher check line patterns.
2. a. square, rectangle
   b. hexagon, triangle
   c. circle, triangle
3. Teacher to check.

Page 24 Assessment

1. a. 1
   b. 5
   c. 3
   d. 1
   e. 4
2. a. square
   b. triangle
   c. circle
   d. oval
   e. hexagon
3. a. oval with nothing inside, oval with nothing inside, oval with sloping lines inside, oval with dots inside
   b. medium-sized circle, small circle, medium-sized circle, small circle
   c. large square, small circle, small square, large circle
4. a. zigzag
   b. sloping
   c. wavy

5.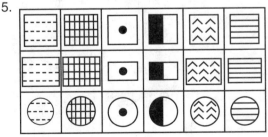

Name	**Date**

1. Draw some shapes that have four sides.

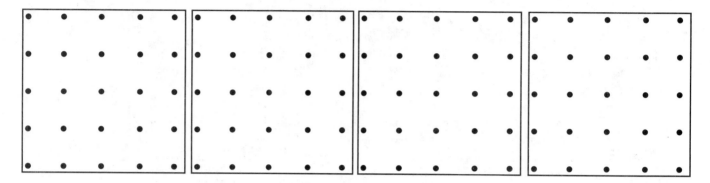

2. How many sides do these shapes have?

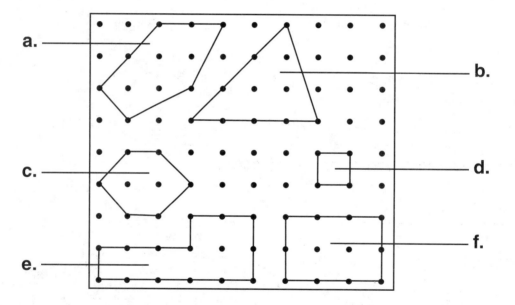

3. **a.** Draw a shape on each geo-board.

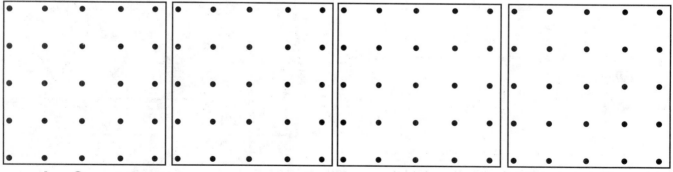

b. Count the sides.

  [ ] sides   [ ] sides   [ ] sides   [ ] sides

Name	**Date**

1. Join the numbers to make shapes.

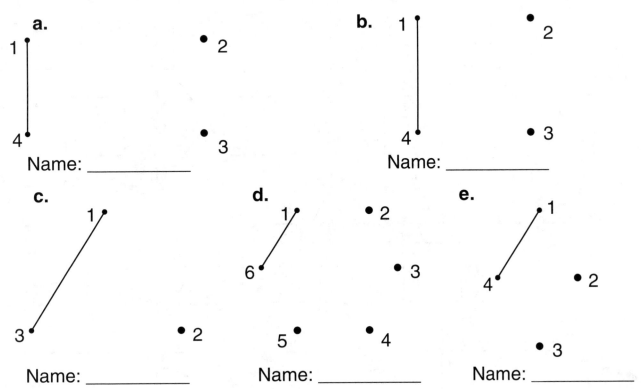

a.

1
4

2
3

Name: _____

b.

1
4

2
3

Name: _____

c.

1
3

2

Name: _____

d.

1
6

2
3

5
4

Name: _____

e.

1
4

2
3

Name: _____

2. Make matching shapes the same color.

© *Teacher Created Resources, Inc.*   *#8991 Targeting Math: Geometry, Chance and Data*

Name	**Date**

1. Color and complete each pattern.

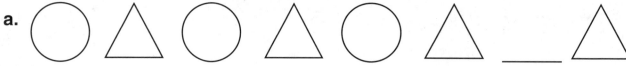

a.

b.

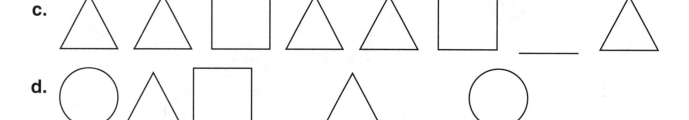

c.

d.

2. Complete the patterns.

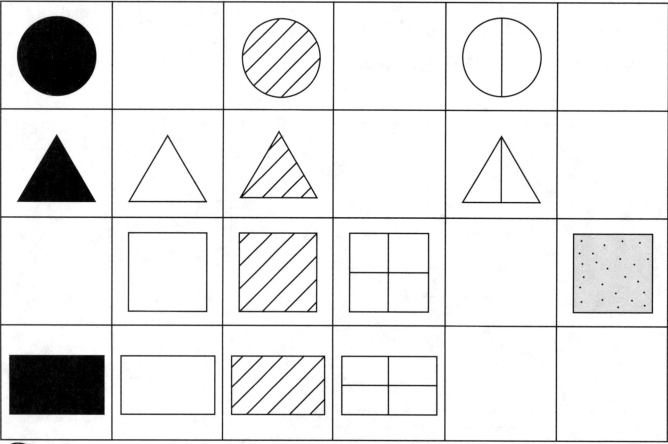

#8991 Targeting Math: Geometry, Chance and Data   © *Teacher Created Resources, Inc.*

Name	**Date**

1. Complete the chart.

Shape	Name	Number of Sides	Number of Corners
a.			
b.			
c. 			
d. 			

2. Color the shapes with three sides red, the shapes with four sides blue, and the shapes with six sides yellow.

3. Circle the shape that has a different number of sides in each row.

a.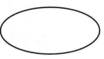

b.

c.

d.

(21)

Name	**Date**

1. Label each line.

| sloping | broken | straight | zigzag | wavy |

a.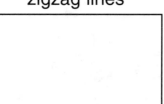

_____

b.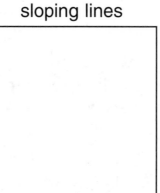

_____

c. _____

_____

d.

_____

e.

_____

2. Decorate these cushions, using the indicated lines. Then color them.

zigzag lines	sloping lines	wavy lines

3. **a.** Decorate this tablecloth with different lines.

        b. What sorts of lines did you use?

_____

_____

_____

_____

_____

_____

_____

_____

     © *Teacher Created Resources, Inc.*

Name	**Date**

1. Complete each pattern.

a.

b.

c. Make your own pattern.

2. Give the names of the two shapes used to make these shapes.

a.    b.    c.

| circle |
| square |
| rectangle |
| triangle |
| hexagon |

_____ _____ _____

_____ _____ _____

3. Make some shapes.

a. Use a circle and a square.

b. Use a triangle and a rectangle.

c. Use a square and a hexagon.

23

Name	**Date**

1. How many sides do these shapes have?

a.    **b.** 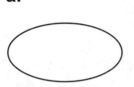   **c.**    **d.** 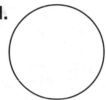   **e.**

_____ _____ _____ _____ _____

2. Name these shapes.

a.    **b.** 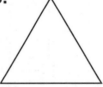   **c.** 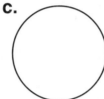   **d.** 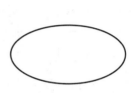   **e.**

_____ _____ _____ _____ _____

3. Complete the patterns.

a.     _____ _____ _____

b.        _____ _____

c. 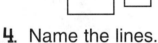 _____ _____ _____ _____ _____

4. Name the lines.

a. 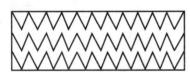   **b.** 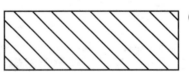   **c.**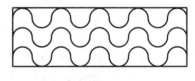

_____ _____ _____

5. Complete the chart.

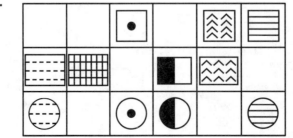

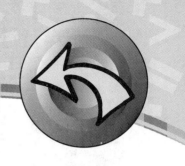

THREE-DIMENSIONAL SHAPES

Three-dimensional shapes are explored through matching identical shapes, finding the shape that is different, and tracing shapes. Shapes are matched to everyday items and are recognized in stacks. Students identify prisms, pyramids, cones, cylinders, faces, edges, and corners. Three-dimensional objects are viewed from different perspectives, and the views are drawn. Skills are practiced by completing diagrams of three-dimensional shapes, drawing shapes and their cross-sections, and completing tables. The activity page involves building with shape blocks and drawing the constructions. Also included is an assessment page with each unit.

© *Teacher Created Resources, Inc.*

BEGINNING 3-D SHAPES

Unit 1

Sorting
Properties
Faces
Edges
Corners

Objectives

- sorts and describes objects in terms of their features, such as size and shape
- classifies objects by a familiar attribute relating to shape
- explores and describes faces, edges, and corners of three-dimensional objects
- describes three-dimensional objects using everyday language, models and sorts them, and recognizes them in drawings
- counts collections up to 10 objects and beyond
- distinguishes between a three-dimensional object and its face

Language

same, shape, three-dimensional, face, corner, edge, stack, model

Materials/Resources

colored pencils, Base 10 materials, other blocks

Contents of Student Pages

- * *Materials needed for each reproducible student page*

Page 28 Identical Shapes
matching solid shapes

Page 29 Shapes That Fit
finding the shape that is different and matching shapes that are the same

Page 30 Tracing Shapes
tracing shapes

Page 31 Matching Shapes
matching shapes with everyday objects

- * *colored pencils*

Page 32 Building Shapes
recognizing shapes in a stack, drawing lines to match shapes, counting blocks in a stack

- * *colored pencils, Base 10 materials*

Page 33 Faces and Corners
identifying faces and corners

Page 34 Assessment
Page 35 Activity—Building a Tower

- * *20 building blocks (2 cylinders and 4 pyramids included)*

Remember

- ❑ *Give students many opportunities to explore two-dimensional and three-dimensional shapes.*
- ❑ *Encourage students to talk about their findings.*

Additional Activities

❑ Give students many opportunities to build models using a variety of objects (e.g., construction sets, woodworking, junk collection).

❑ Make a ramp with a length of wood and provide students with a variety of objects, (e.g., tins or boxes). Let them experiment and find out which will roll and which will slide.

❑ Give students opportunities to sort, compare, and classify three-dimensional objects.

❑ Make buildings out of shoeboxes or plastic ice-cream containers for students to display and discuss three-dimensional shapes used in each model.

❑ Display and discuss different three-dimensional shapes in foods.

❑ Provide opportunities for the students to draw around three-dimensional shapes.

❑ Allow students to find three-dimensional shapes in magazines and cut them out. Have students sort and paste them in a class book.

❑ Have a shape table for a week (e.g., cylinders). Encourage students to bring a shape from home.

Answers

Page 28 Identical Shapes

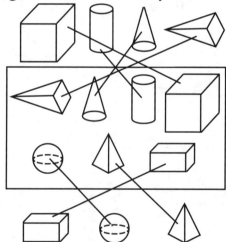

Page 29 Shapes That Fit

1. a. Third shape from the left
   b. Third shape from the left
   c. Fourth shape from the left
2.

Page 30 Tracing Shapes
Make sure all shapes are traced.

Page 31 Matching Shapes

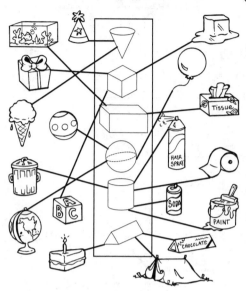

Page 32 Building Shapes
1. Make sure shapes are joined.
   a. 3
   b. 3
   c. 4
   d. 10
2. a. 5
   b. 2
   c. 6
   d. c
3. a. 3
   b. 5
   c. 5
   d. a

Page 33 Faces and Corners
1. a. 3, 3, 6
   b. 3, 3, 6
2. a. 4, 1, 5
   b. 5, 0, 5

Page 34 Assessment
1. a. Third shape from the left
   b. Fourth shape from the left
2. a. 5
   b. 6
3. a. 8
   b. 6
4. sphere/balloon, rectangular prism/tissue box, cylinder/soda can, cube/jack-in-the-box, cone/party hat

© Teacher Created Resources, Inc.

Name	**Date**

Join the objects that are the same.

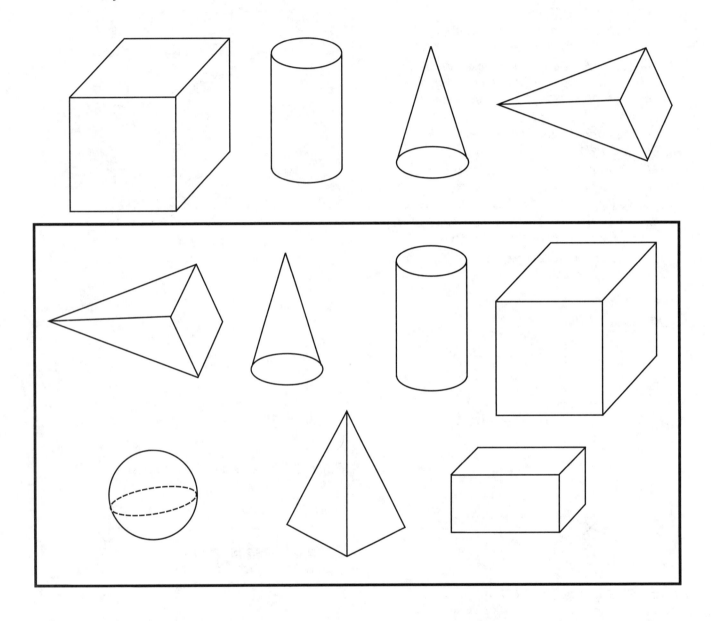

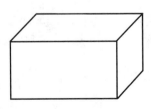 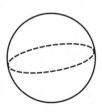 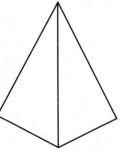

Name	**Date**

1. Circle the shape in each row that does not belong.

a.

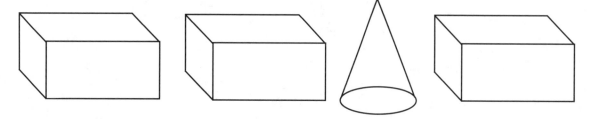

b.

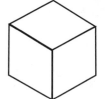 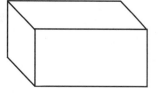 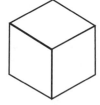

c.

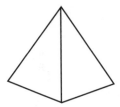 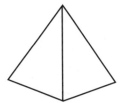 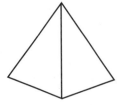 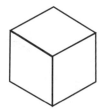

2. Draw a line from each object to where it fits into the puzzle.

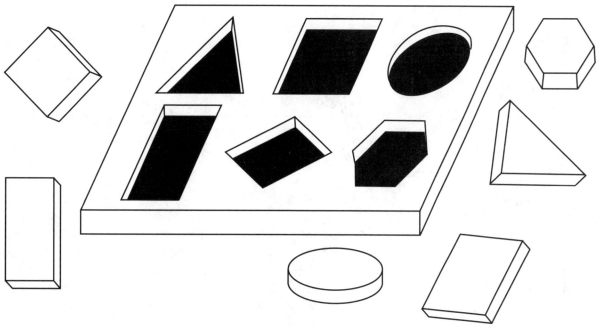

© *Teacher Created Resources, Inc.*

#8991 Targeting Math: Geometry, Chance and Data

Name	**Date**

Trace the shapes.

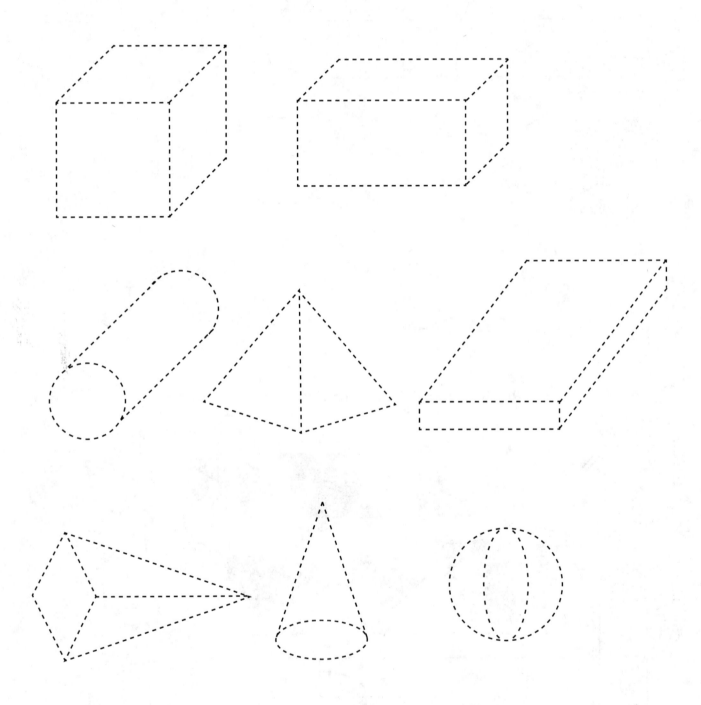

#8991 Targeting Math: Geometry, Chance and Data © *Teacher Created Resources, Inc.*

Name	**Date**

Draw lines from the objects to the shapes. Use a different color for each shape.

© *Teacher Created Resources, Inc.*　　　　　　　*#8991 Targeting Math: Geometry, Chance and Data*

Name	**Date**

1. Sally made these buildings. Join the matching shapes. Use different colors.

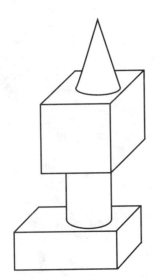 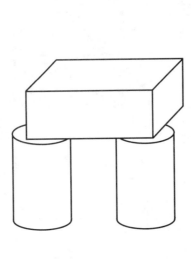 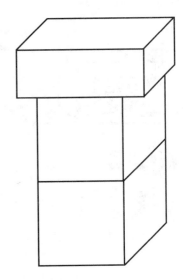

    a. How many cubes did she use? _____

    b. How many cylinders did she use? _____

    c. How many different shapes did she use? _____

    d. How many blocks did she use altogether? _____

2. Count the blocks in each stack. Write the number on the line.

  a. 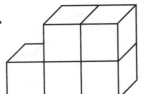 _____   **b.** 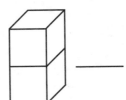 _____   **c.** 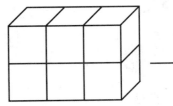 _____

    d. Which model is the biggest? _____

3. Count the blocks in each stack. Write the number on the line.

  a. 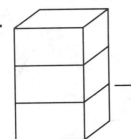 _____   **b.** 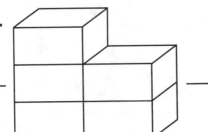 _____   **c.**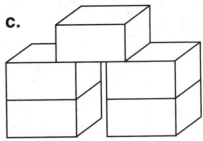

32 **d.** Which model is the smallest? _____   _____

Name	**Date**

1. Put a big dot on each face you can see.

   a.

   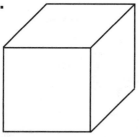

   How many faces can you see? _____

   How many faces are hidden? _____

   How many faces altogether? _____

   b.

   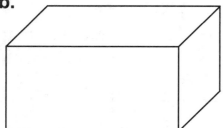

   How many faces can you see? _____

   How many faces are hidden? _____

   How many faces altogether? _____

2. Put a dot on each corner you can see.

   a.

   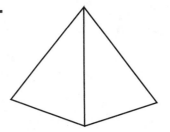

   How many corners can you see? _____

   How many corners are hidden? _____

   How many corners altogether? _____

   b.

   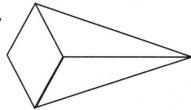

   How many corners can you see? _____

   How many corners are hidden? _____

   How many corners altogether? _____

33

Name	**Date**

1. Circle the shape in each row that is different.

a.

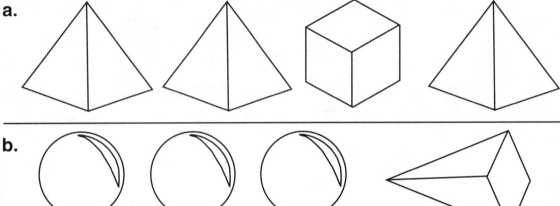

b.

2. Put a dot on each face you can see. Under each shape, write how many faces there are altogether.

a.

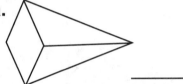
_____

b.

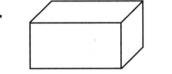
_____

3. Put a dot on each corner you can see. Under each shape, write how many corners there are altogether.

a.

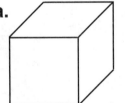
_____

b.

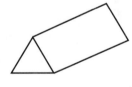
_____

4. Draw a line from each object to its shape.

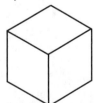
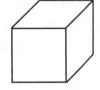

SODA   Tissue

Name	Date

You will need 20 building blocks.

You must have 2 cylinders and 4 pyramids.

Build the tallest tower you can and then draw it in the box.

© *Teacher Created Resources, Inc.*

MORE 3-D SHAPES

Unit 2

Properties of three-dimensional shapes
Sorting three-dimensional shapes
Faces, edges, and corners

Objectives

- names mathematical shapes which can be found as components of familiar things
- sorts and describes objects in terms of their features such as size and shape
- explores and describes faces, edges, and corners of three-dimensional objects
- investigates and describes objects from different points of view
- distinguishes between a three-dimensional object and its face
- makes stacking and packing patterns of three-dimensional objects that will stack or pack

Language

cube, prism, cone, pyramid, sphere, cylinder, slide, roll, stack, curved, flat, edge, corner, face, surface, matrix

Materials/Resources

a set of classroom solid shapes; a collection of everyday objects to represent solid shapes; blocks (cube-shaped), scissors, glue

Contents of Student Pages

- * Materials needed for each reproducible student page

Page 38 Identify Shapes
identify and recognize solid shapes

Page 39 Solid Shapes
investigate the properties of solid shapes, classifying by size and pattern

- * scissors, glue

Page 40 Faces, Edges, and Corners
understanding the relationship of two-dimensional shapes to three-dimensional objects

- * solid shapes

Page 41 Cubes
looking at cubes from different perspectives (e.g., top view and side view; impact of movement on perspective)

- * small cubes

Page 42 Faces
relationship of faces to changing three-dimensional shapes, using patterns to predict outcomes

Page 43 Building
applying logical sequences to obtain maximum variations; drawing three-dimensional shapes; understanding properties of spheres

- * cubes, three-dimensional shapes

Page 44 Assessment

- * 1-minute timer, three-dimensional shaped blocks

Remember

Use three-dimensional materials in a wide variety of free play activities, including arranging, building, packing, spinning, sorting, filling, and emptying. The teacher should discuss categories chosen for sorting activities and encourage children to note attributes of size, shape, uses, and movement.

Additional Activities

- ❏ *Identify shapes by touch. Put shapes into a box. Students take turns to close their eyes, put a hand in the box, and describe a shape before pulling it out.*
- ❏ *Painting all faces of shapes and counting them. Paint each face a different color.*
- ❏ *Play an "I spy" game using shapes in the classroom.*
- ❏ *Cover a desktop with a variety of shapes from the classroom. Answer questions. How many shapes? Which shape covered the most surface?*
- ❏ *Make shape dominoes using three-dimensional shapes.*
- ❏ *Make three-dimensional shapes from modeling clay.*

Answers

Page 38 Identify Shapes

1. Make sure each object corresponds with its shape name.

2.

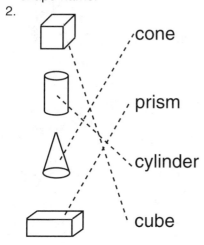

3. 8, 4, 0, 3

Page 39 Solid Shapes

Row 1: cone

Row 2: cylinder

Row 3: lined circle

Row 4: dark gray cube

Page 40 Faces, Edges, and Corners

1. 6, 12, 8
   3, 2, 0
   1, 0, 0

2. The cylinder, triangular prism, and the rectangular prism should be circled.

Page 41 Cubes

1. 27, 64

2. a.   b.

3.

Page 42 Faces

1. 2, 4, 6

2. The second, third, and fourth shape from the left should be circled.

3. a. square
   b. circle
   c. circle

Page 43 Building

1. Make sure each model has only 4 cubes.
2. Make sure each tower is constructed.
3. Spheres do not have any sides on which you can build.

Page 44 Assessment

1. Make sure the three objects do not have any curved surfaces.
2. cube
3. 10, 4, 2
4. a.

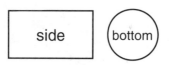

b.

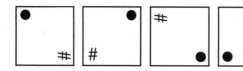

5.

6.

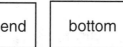

cylinder

prism

sphere

cube

7. Teacher to check.

37

© Teacher Created Resources, Inc.

Name	**Date**

1. Draw 4 things that are shaped like the item on the left.

2. Join each shape to its name.   3. This is Billy's building.

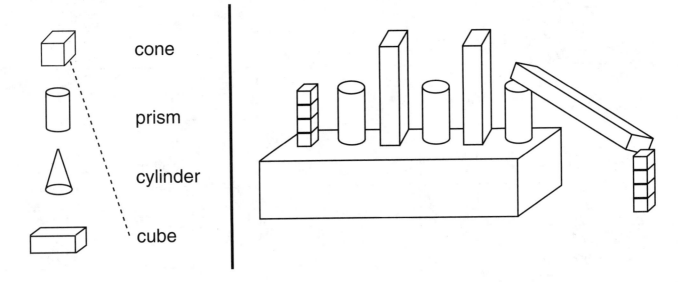

cone

prism

cylinder

cube

How many of each shape are in Billy's building?

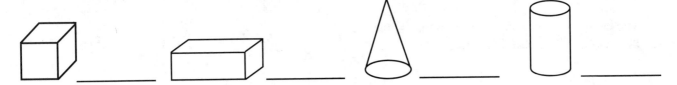

#8991 Targeting Math: Geometry, Chance and Data   *© Teacher Created Resources, Inc.*

Name **Date**

Cut out the shapes below and glue them in the correct space to complete the matrix pattern.

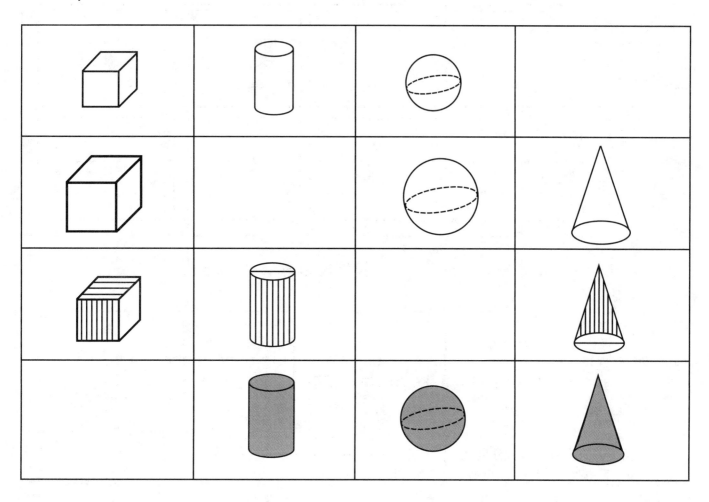

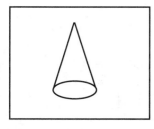
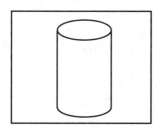
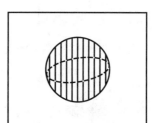
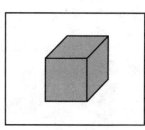

© *Teacher Created Resources, Inc.*

Name		**Date**

1. Complete the table. Use shapes to help you.

	faces 6	edges 12	corners 8

2. Kylie has been printing with shapes. This is the pattern she made. Circle the shapes she used to make this pattern.

Kylie's Printing Pattern

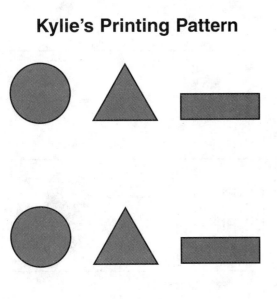

Shapes

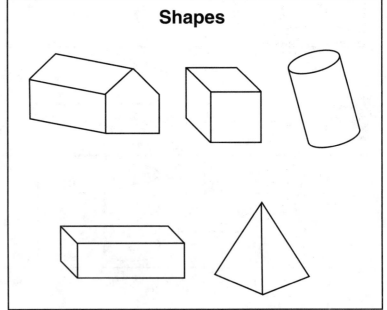

Name	**Date**

1. One cube is shown below. Next to the cube is a larger cube made of 8 small cubes.

 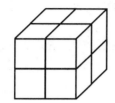

   Predict how many cubes you need to make a larger cube _____ and an even larger cube _____ . Check your answers.

2. Here is an alphabet block with pictures on each face.

   a. Draw the picture you would see from the top view.

   b. Draw the pictures you would see from the side views.

   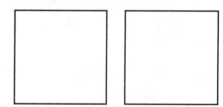

3. Draw what you would see if you rolled it once to the left.

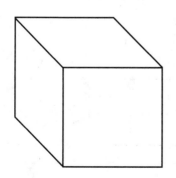  

Name   **Date**

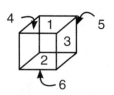

If this block was dipped in a can of paint, 6 faces would be covered.

1. If these blocks were stuck together, how many faces would be covered?

a. 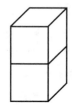 **b.** 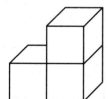 **c.**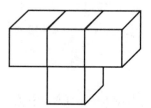

_____ _____ _____

2. Circle the shapes that would have a <u>circular face</u> if cut through on the dashed line.

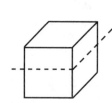 (a curved ball)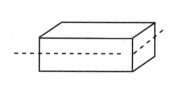

3. Color the cross-section you would see if the shapes were cut along the dashed line.

a.					
b.					
c.					

#8991 Targeting Math: Geometry, Chance and Data   © *Teacher Created Resources, Inc.*

Name	**Date**

1. Take 4 cubes and make 4 different models. Draw each one.

2. How many different towers can you make with these 3 blocks?

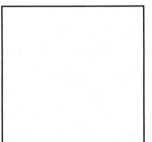   

Draw your constructions.

a.	**b.**	**c.**

3. Explain why we haven't used spheres.

_____

_____

43

Name	**Date**

1. Draw 3 objects that do not have a curved surface.

2. What am I? I have 6 faces. You can build with me. I have edges and corners.

_____

3. If you had to paint the inside and the outside of these containers, how many faces would you paint?

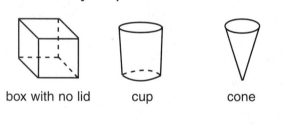

box with no lid   cup   cone

_____   _____   _____

4. Draw in the shapes of the missing faces.

Example:

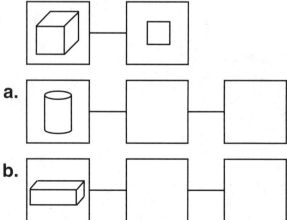

a.

b.

5. Draw the pattern you will see from the front when you roll this cube to the right 4 times.

1st time   2nd time   3rd time   4th time

6. Match the shapes to their names.

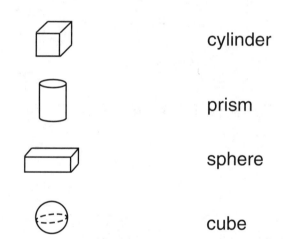

cylinder

prism

sphere

cube

7. You will need a 1-minute timer and 10 blocks. Build a tower and draw the blocks you used.

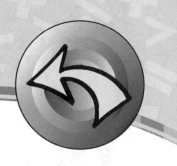

POSITION AND MAPPING/ TRANSFORMATION

The Position and Mapping unit uses the language of position in a number of different exercises. Students follow directions to complete drawings, and answer questions from drawings. They find their way through mazes and draw paths on a map. One assessment page is included. A fun activity page has students moving skinny dogs and fat cats to different positions.

In the Transformation unit, pattern blocks are used to make patterns. Mirrors are used to explore and aid in the drawing of reflections. Flipping, sliding, and turning are practiced when patterns are created. Changing shape is explored through bending and stretching. There is one assessment page.

© *Teacher Created Resources, Inc.*

POSITION AND MAPPING

Unit 1

Over & under
Left & right
Positions
Views
Mapping

Objectives

- uses everyday language associated with position
- uses and understands the language of position
- represents the position of objects using pictures, sketches, and models, and uses everyday language to describe their position
- describes the location of an object in relation to other objects
- finds paths on simple maps and mazes

Language

above, back-to-back, backward, behind, below, between, bottom, face-to-face, forward, front, furthest, in front of, inside, left, longer, map, maze, middle, next to, on, on the bottom of, on top of, outside, over, path, right, row, shorter, shortest, side, taller, top, under view, viewpoints

Materials/Resources

writing/drawing materials, cubes, colored pencils

Contents of Student Pages

- ✱ Materials needed for each reproducible student page

Page 48 Over and Under
illustrating and circling position words

Page 49 Left and Right
circling the correct position word; reading and drawing the correct position

Page 50 Different Positions
following instructions; using a picture to answer questions
- ✱ colored pencils

Page 51 Positions! Positions!
drawing and coloring using position; circling the correct positional word; using a picture to answer questions on position
- ✱ colored pencils

Page 52 Different Views
building models and sketching different views
- ✱ cubes

Page 53 Mapping
finding way through mazes, drawing shortest path on map, using a map to answer questions

Page 54 Assessment
- ✱ cubes

Page 55 Activity—Where Do They Live?
writing directions to get to a person's house using left and right

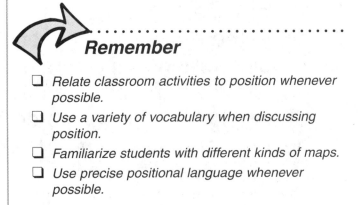

Remember

- ❏ Relate classroom activities to position whenever possible.
- ❏ Use a variety of vocabulary when discussing position.
- ❏ Familiarize students with different kinds of maps.
- ❏ Use precise positional language whenever possible.

© Teacher Created Resources, Inc.

Additional Activities

❑ *Conduct a treasure hunt using positional instructions. Students can read or listen to a set of instructions and find the "treasure."*

❑ *Build models. Discuss/draw/write about them.*

❑ *Label pictures/posters using positional sentences.*

❑ *Play "Pairs." One student says/writes positional instructions and the partner follows instructions.*

❑ *Draw a map and write questions about it using positional words.*

❑ *Choose a picture book. Retell or rewrite the story using positional language.*

❑ *Practice marching. (Good for learning left and right.)*

Answers

Page 48 Over and Under

1. a. Make sure there is a star over the moon.
   b. Make sure there is an egg under the hen.
2. a. over
   b. over
   c. under
   d. under
3. a. yes
   b. no

Page 49 Left and Right

1. a. right
   b. left
   c. left
   d. right
2. a. right
   b. left
3. a. Make sure a spoon is drawn to the left of the fork.
   b. Make sure a moon is drawn to the right of the sun.
   c. Make sure a bone is drawn to the left of the dog.
   d. Make sure a worm is drawn to the left of the fish.

Page 50 Different Positions

1. a. Make sure the taller tree is colored red.
   b. Make sure the longer pencil is colored green.
   c. Make sure the shorter snake is colored blue.
   d. Make sure the bigger boat is colored brown.
2. a. Make sure a person is drawn next to the palm tree.
   b. Make sure a crab is drawn next to the person.
   c. Make sure fish are drawn swimming in front of the island.
   d. Make sure a bird is drawn flying above the tree.
   e. Make sure a boat is drawn in the water below the sun.

Page 51 Positions! Positions!

1. a. Make sure a cloud is drawn above a tree.
   b. Make sure a mountain is drawn behind a house.
2. a. outside
   b. back-to-back
3. a. fish or cloud
   b. rocks, water, or tree
   c. rocks or water
   d. cloud

Page 52 Different Viewpoints

1.

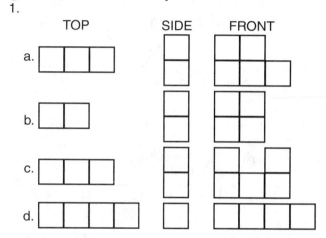

2. Teacher to check.

Page 53 Mapping

1. Teacher check mazes.
2. Line should be drawn from school, left on Third Road, right on Long Street, then right on Jones Street into the home.
3. a. First Rd.
   b. Jones St.
   c. Third Rd., Long St.
   d. Busy St., Second St.

Page 54 Assessment

1. a. over
   b. on the bottom
   c. left
2. a. Make sure the girl is to the right of the tree and below a cloud.
   b. Make sure a car is next to a house and in front of a mountain.
3. Teacher to check.

Page 55 Activity—Where Do They Live?

1. 2nd on the right
2. 4th on the right
3. 1st on the left
4. 1st on the right
5. 2nd on the left
6. 3rd on the left
7. 4th on the left
8. 3rd on the right

Name	**Date**

1. Read and draw.

a. A star over the moon	**b.** An egg under the hen

2. Circle the right word.

a. The ball is (over / under) the bat.	**b.** The rabbit is (over / under) the grass.

c. The leaf is (over / under) the frog.	**d.** The snake is (over / under) the car.

3. Answer *yes* or *no*.

a. The hat is on top of the head.	**b.** The sea is on top of the boat.

_____	_____

#8991 Targeting Math: Geometry, Chance and Data   © *Teacher Created Resources, Inc.*

Name	**Date**

1. Which side is colored in? Circle the correct answer.

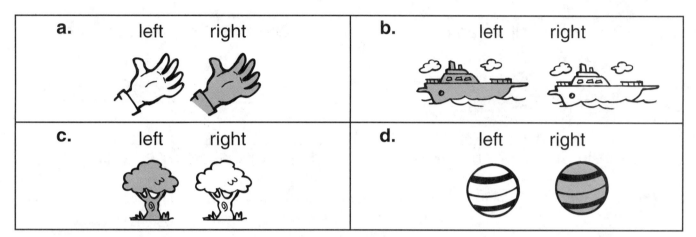

a. left　　right	**b.** left　　right
c. left　　right	**d.** left　　right

2. Answer these using *left* or *right*.

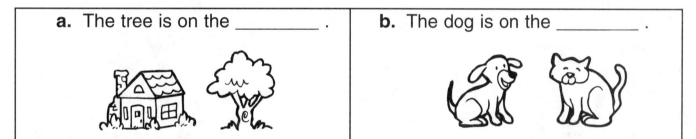

a. The tree is on the _____ .	**b.** The dog is on the _____ .

3. Draw:

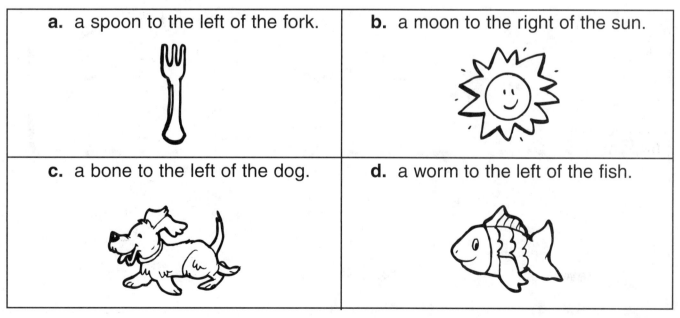

a. a spoon to the left of the fork.	**b.** a moon to the right of the sun.
c. a bone to the left of the dog.	**d.** a worm to the left of the fish.

© *Teacher Created Resources, Inc.*
#8991 Targeting Math: Geometry, Chance and Data

Name	**Date**

1. Complete.

a. Color the taller tree red.	**b.** Color the longer pencil green.
c. Color the shorter snake blue.	**d.** Color the bigger boat brown.

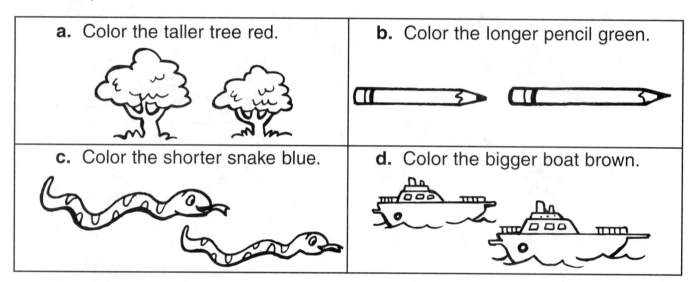

2. Complete the instructions using the picture below.

   a. Draw a person next to the palm tree.

   b. Draw a crab next to the person.

   c. Draw fish swimming in front of the island.

   d. Draw a bird flying above the tree.

   e. Draw a boat in the water below the sun.

Name	**Date**

1. Draw and color.

a. a cloud above a tree	**b.** a mountain behind a house

2. Circle the correct word.

a. The car is (inside / outside) the garage. 	**b.** The people are (face-to-face / back-to-back). 

3. Use the picture to answer the questions.

a. What is to the right of the tree and to the left of the waterfall? _____

b. What is between the fish and the girl? _____

c. What is below the sun and to the left of the girl? _____

d. What is next to the tree and above the waterfall? _____

© *Teacher Created Resources, Inc.*

#8991 Targeting Math: Geometry, Chance and Data

Name	**Date**

1. Build these models from cubes if you need help. Draw the different views.

a.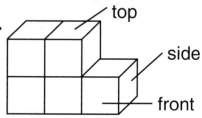

Top	Side	Front

b.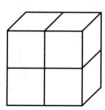

Top	Side	Front

c.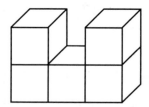

Top	Side	Front

d.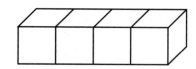

Top	Side	Front

2. Using cubes, build a model. Draw its top, side, and front views.

Top	Side	Front

#8991 Targeting Math: Geometry, Chance and Data
© *Teacher Created Resources, Inc.*

| **Name** | **Date** |

1. Find your way through these mazes.

a.

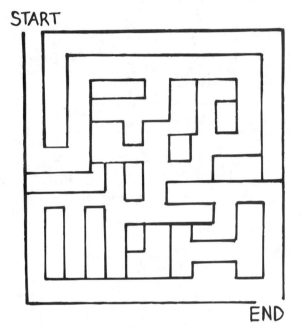

b.

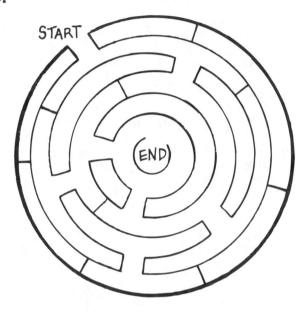

2. Draw the shortest path on the map to get from school to home.

3. Use the map above to answer these questions.

   a. On which street is the entrance to the park? _____

   b. On which street is "home"? _____

   c. On which streets are the school? _____

   _____

   d. Name the streets that pass the church. _____

   _____

53

Name	**Date**

1. Circle the correct word.

   a. The ruler is (under / over) the book.

   b. The crown is (on the bottom / on the top) of the hand.

   c. The tree is on the (right / left).

2. Read and draw.

a. A girl to the right of a tree and below a cloud	**b.** A car next to a house and in front of a mountain

3. Build a model using cubes. Draw the top, side, and front views.

Top	Side	Front

54

Name	**Date**

Write the directions to get from the "X" to each person's house. The first one has been done for you.

Sally

Pete

Pam

Clay

Cam

Tamara

Billy

Jane

X *You are here*

⟵ *Left*   *Right* ⟶

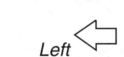

1. <u>2nd</u> on the <u>right</u>   5. ____ on the _____

2. ____ on the _____   6. ____ on the _____

3. ____ on the _____   7. ____ on the _____

4. ____ on the _____   8. ____ on the _____

(55)

TRANSFORMATION

Unit 2

Patterns
Flip
Slide
Turn
Reflect

Objectives

- makes a decorative pattern
- makes symmetrical patterns
- uses and understands the language of movement
- generates patterns and follows rules based on the simple repetition and movement of things
- repeats, orients, and turns over things when making patterns

Language

bend, changing, flip, mirror patterns, pattern block, patterns, reflection, repeat, shapes, slide, stretch, symmetrical, symmetry, trace, turn

Materials/Resources

writing/drawing materials, pattern blocks, mirrors, 50¢ coins, objects in classroom, colored pencils

Contents of Student Pages

* Materials needed for each reproducible student page

Page 58 Patterns

tracing around pattern blocks to make patterns

* pattern blocks, colored pencils

Page 59 Symmetry

mirror patterns and completing a picture using reflection

* mirrors, colored pencils

Page 60 Changing Shapes

stretching balloons, stretching elastic, and things that stretch and bend

* colored pencils

Page 61 Slides

sliding pattern blocks and other objects to make patterns

* pattern blocks, colored pencils, objects in classroom

Page 62 Turns

turning pattern blocks to make patterns

* pattern blocks

Page 63 Flips

flipping pattern blocks and objects to make pictures and patterns; flipping a 50¢ coin

* pattern blocks, flat objects in classroom

Page 64 Assessment

* mirrors, pattern blocks

Remember

- ❏ Use precise language when discussing transformations.
- ❏ Note the different kinds of patterns in the environment.
- ❏ Pattern blocks can be replaced by cardboard templates.

56

Additional Activities

❑ *Make a picture by tracing around pattern blocks. Write or tell a story about it.*

❑ *Complete tangram pictures. Write or tell stories about them.*

❑ *Find patterns in the environment. List/draw them.*

❑ *Make blob paintings (for symmetry).*

❑ *Find lines of symmetry in the environment.*

❑ *Find evidence of flipping, sliding, and turning in the environment.*

❑ *List/draw as many things as you can that stretch, bend, or change shape in some way.*

Answers

Page 58 Patterns

Teacher to check.

Page 59 Symmetry

1. a.

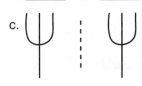

b.

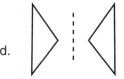

c.

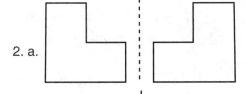

d.

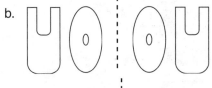

2. a.

b.

c.

d.

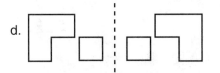

3.

Page 60 Changing Shapes

1. a. Teacher to check.
   b. It enlarged.
   c. It will get smaller again.
2. a. Teacher to check.
   b. Because the elastic stretched, the word did, too.
3. Stretch: rubber band, chewing gum, jeans, balloon

   Bend: coat hanger, paper, tree

Page 61 Slides

Teacher to check.

Page 62 Turns

Teacher to check.

Page 63 Flips

1.

2.

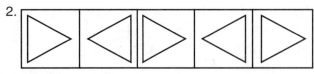

3. Teacher to check.
4. Teacher to check.

Page 64 Assessment

1. Teacher to check.
2. Teacher to check.
3. Teacher to check.
4. a.

   b.

5.

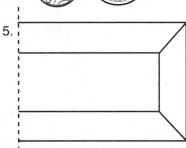

Name	**Date**

1. Choose a pattern block. Trace around it to make a pattern across the page.

2. Choose another pattern block. Make another pattern across the page.

3. Choose 2 or 3 pattern blocks. Trace around them to make a pattern.

#8991 Targeting Math: Geometry, Chance and Data   © *Teacher Created Resources, Inc.*

Name	**Date**

1. Draw the mirror patterns.

   a.

   b.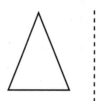

   c.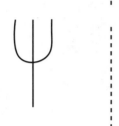

   d.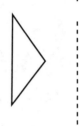

2. Now try these.

   a.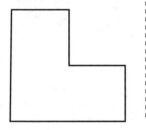

   b.

   c.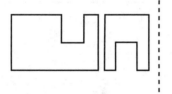

   d.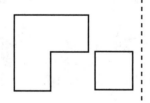

3. Finish the reflection. Color it.

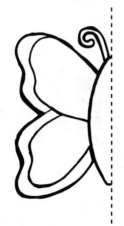

© *Teacher Created Resources, Inc.*

#8991 Targeting Math: Geometry, Chance and Data

Name	**Date**

1. The balloon below
   has not been blown
   up. It has a picture on
   it.

   a. Draw what the
   picture looks like
   once it has been
   blown up.

   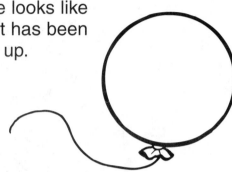

   b. What happened? _____

   _____

   c. What will happen to the picture when air is let out?

   _____

2. Here is some elastic with something written on it.

   a. Draw what will happen if it is stretched.

school	

   b. Why do you think this happened?

   _____

3. Color the things that *stretch*. Circle the things that bend.

#8991 Targeting Math: Geometry, Chance and Data   © Teacher Created Resources, Inc.

Name	**Date**

1. Choose a pattern block. Trace around it. Slide it and trace around it again. Continue this across the page.

2. A pattern block has been traced. Continue the sliding to make a pattern.

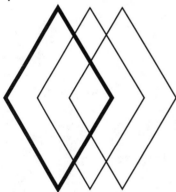

3. Find 2 small objects in your classroom. Trace around them and slide them across the page to make a pattern.

© *Teacher Created Resources, Inc.*   *#8991 Targeting Math: Geometry, Chance and Data*

Name	**Date**

1. The following tiles have been turned. Continue turning them to make a pattern.

    a. 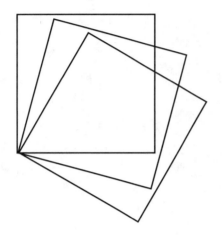   **b.**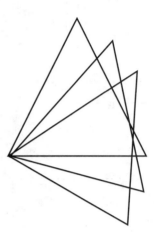

2. Choose a pattern block. Trace around it. Turn it and trace around it again. Continue until you make a pattern.

Name	**Date**

1. This shape has been flipped. Continue the pattern.

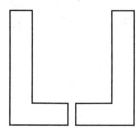

2. Flip a triangle across the page. The pattern has been started for you.

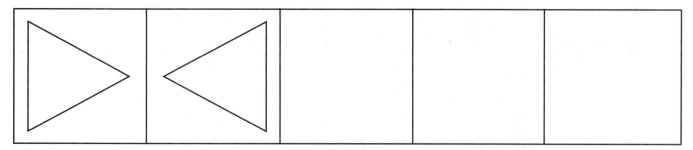

3. Find a flat object in your classroom. Trace around it and flip it across the page.

4. Draw your own shape in the first box. Flip it across the page.

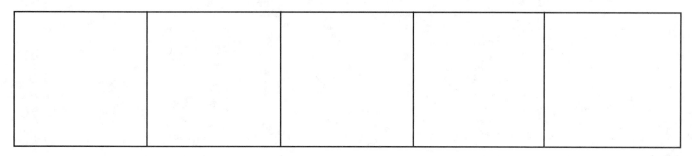

© *Teacher Created Resources, Inc.*

Name	**Date**

1. Choose a pattern block. Draw it. Flip, slide, and turn it in the spaces below.

   Pattern Block   Flip   Slide   Turn

2. Name 3 things that stretch.

   _____

3. Name 3 things that bend.

   _____

4. Draw these mirror patterns.

   a.    **b.**

5. Finish the reflection.

   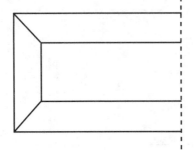

GRAPHS

The skills of recording, summarizing, representing, and organizing data are used in these two units on graphs. Students count objects to answer questions. They cut out and order objects, and also draw simple objects to make graphs. Conducting surveys and then using the data to draw graphs is introduced. Students must interpret and locate information using picture and column graphs. The tally method of recording and collecting data is also contained in these units. The activity page is a fun graph that is interpreted to answer questions. One assessment page is included in each unit.

BEGINNING GRAPHS

Unit 1

Surveys
Interpreting graphs
Drawing graphs
Gathering information

Objectives

- counts collections up to 10 objects and beyond
- recognizes and compares the sizes of groups through a variety of strategies such as estimating, matching, one to one and counting
- sorts and describes in terms of their features such as size and shape
- makes simple pictographs using one to one correspondence between real data and a representation
- participates in classifying and sequencing objects or pictures
- compares groups using pictorial representations
- selects and carries out the operation appropriate to situations involving addition and subtraction
- displays and summarizes data based on one-to-one correspondence between data and representation
- compares groups using objects to represent other groups
- displays objects and pictures and describes data in words and numbers

Language

compare, more, less, same, equal, count, one-ten, how many, altogether, graph, key, add, take away, total, column, least, counters, most popular, least popular

Materials/Resources

colored pencils, scissors, glue, materials such as counters or plastic cubes for finding data, pencil, eraser, grid paper

Contents of Student Pages

* Materials needed for each reproducible student page

Page 68 Counting Objects
counting objects and items in a graph, answering graph questions

* colored pencils

Page 69 Interpreting Information
cutting to sort, gluing to make a graph relating to size

* scissors, glue

Page 70 Using Information
answering questions about a graph

* colored pencils

Page 71 Interpreting a Graph
answering questions, drawing own graph

* red and green colored pencils

Page 72 Answering Questions
counting objects and transferring the information

* colored pencils

Page 73 Making a Graph
drawing a graph from class data and interpreting a graph

Page 74 Assessment
* colored pencils

Page 75 Activity—Dinner Time
reading and answering questions about a graph

....
Remember

Before starting ensure each student:

- ❑ has a sharp pencil.
- ❑ has an understanding that graphs can represent objects.
- ❑ has many experiences of a concrete nature before they progress to more abstract graphs.

Additional Activities

❑ Provide many opportunities for students to sort and compare objects according to shape, size, and other features with items such as counters, buttons, or beads.

❑ Provide opportunities for students to recognize and compare the size of groups through a variety of strategies such as matching, one-to-one correspondence, and counting.

❑ Model appropriate language (e.g., more, less, same, or equal) in all key learning areas so students can develop the appropriate language of comparison. Use comparison situations that arise naturally within the class. (e.g., "Who watched a particular TV program?" or "Who went to the movies?") Encourage students to make suggestions.

❑ As a class, make pictorial representations of different surveys (e.g., our pets, growth rates of plants, ways of traveling to school, our birthdays, hair color, eye color, colors we like). Put them on display.

❑ Take as many opportunities as possible to develop the idea of organizing information that can be easily interpreted.

❑ Read stories like Eric Carle's *The Very Hungry Caterpillar*. Students can draw the items of food and compare the groups. Later, information such as this can be used to make simple graphs.

❑ Provide lots of opportunities for the students to use concrete objects to represent objects (e.g., cubes or counters) when counting objects in a group and then graphing.

❑ Provide many opportunities for students to make simple graphs with your guidance, using drawings, cutouts, stickers, pictures from magazines, sticky squares, or dots.

Answers

Page 68 Counting Objects
1. a. 8
   b. 2
   c. 4
   d. 3
   e. 6
2. a. Make sure cars are colored correctly.
   b. 5, 2, 4, 1
   c. 12
   d. green

Page 69 Interpreting Information
1. Make sure bears are colored.
2. Make sure bears are glued in their correct places.
3. a. 4
   b. 6
   c. 10

Page 70 Using Information
1. Make sure pencils are colored correctly.
2. 4, 5, 3, 6
3. 3
4. 4
5. 1
6. 1
7. 18

Page 71 Interpreting a Graph
1. 9, 4
2. a. Answers will vary.
   b. Check to make sure the results in the graph match the number of apples colored in letter a.

Page 72 Answering Questions
1. Make sure flowers are colored correctly.
2. 4, 2, 3, 1
3. a. red
   b. 1
   c. 10
   d. 2
   e. 3
4. Make sure there are 4 flowers colored red, 2 flowers colored purple, 3 flowers colored yellow, and 1 flower colored orange.

Page 73 Making a Graph
1. Answers will vary for graph.
2. a. 8
   b. 4
   c. pear
   d. apple
   e. 21
   f. 1

Page 74 Assessment
1. a. 4
   b. 2
2. Circle first row.
3. Make sure cupcakes are colored correctly.
4. a. blue
   b. red
   c. 9
   d. 1
   e. 1

Page 75 Activity—Dinner Time
1. Sunday
2. Thursday
3. stir-fried snails
4. Friday because she didn't eat much or Sunday because she ate too much.
5. Answers will vary.

Name	Date

1. Count the objects.

   a.

   b.

   c.

   d.

   e.

2. **a.** Color the cars.

Peter's Cars

yellow	red	blue	green

   b. How many cars are:

   yellow? _____   red? _____   blue? _____   green? _____

   c. How many cars altogether? _____

   d. There are more __red__ cars than _____ cars.

68

| Name | Date |

1. Color the bears.

2. Cut out the bears and glue them onto the graph.

Small						
Big						

3. **a.** How many small bears? _____

    b. How many big bears? _____

    c. How many bears altogether? _____

 ....

© *Teacher Created Resources, Inc.*   *#8991 Targeting Math: Geometry, Chance and Data*

Name	**Date**

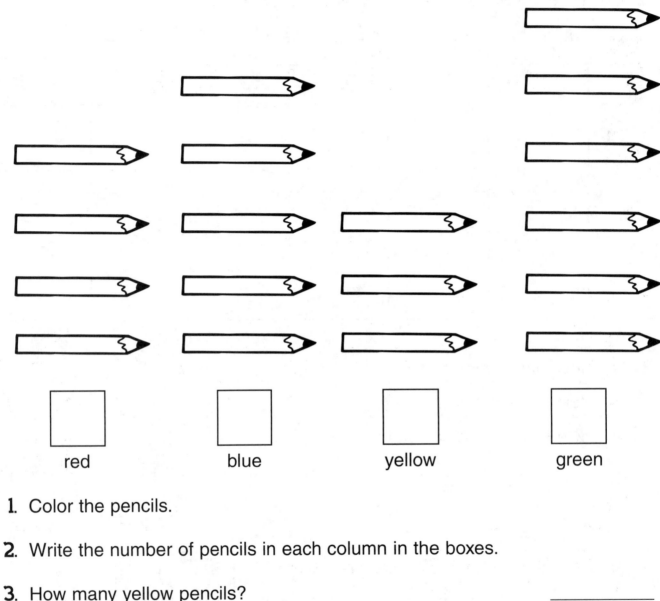

red   blue   yellow   green

1. Color the pencils.

2. Write the number of pencils in each column in the boxes.

3. How many yellow pencils?   _____

4. How many red pencils?   _____

5. How many more blue pencils are there than red pencils?   _____

6. How many more green pencils are there than blue pencils?   _____

7. How many pencils altogether?   _____

#8991 Targeting Math: Geometry, Chance and Data   © Teacher Created Resources, Inc.

Name	**Date**

1. Lee counted some apples and made this graph.

X	X	X	X	X	X	X	X	X			

red

X	X	X	X								

green   Lee had _____ red apples and _____ green apples.

2. **a.** Color some apples green and some red.

b. Draw a graph of the apples you colored.

red

green

71

Name　　　　　　　　　　　　　　　　**Date**

Flowers in the Vase

| Total: | Total: | Total: | Total: |

red　　　　　　　　purple　　　　　　　　yellow　　　　　　　　orange

1. Color the flowers below the graph the correct color.

2. Count the flowers in each column and write in the totals.

3. **a.** Most flowers are _____ in color.

   b. How many orange flowers? _____

   c. How many flowers altogether? _____

   d. How many more yellow flowers than orange
   flowers? _____

   e. How many more red flowers than orange flowers?

   _____

4. Color the flowers in the vase to match the colors in
   the graph.

#8991 Targeting Math: Geometry, Chance and Data　　　　　　© *Teacher Created Resources, Inc.*

Name	**Date**

1. Make a graph to show the number of children in your class who wear glasses.

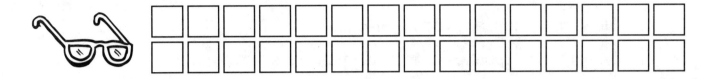

_____ children wear glasses

_____ children don't wear glasses

2. This graph shows fruit eaten for lunch.

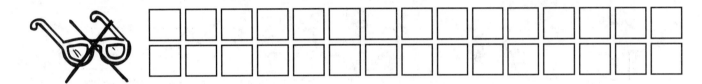

a. How many apples were eaten? _____

b. How many oranges were eaten? _____

c. What was the least poplar fruit? _____

d. What was the most popular fruit? _____

e. How many pieces of fruit were eaten altogether? _____

f. How many more oranges than pears were eaten? _____

73

Name	Date

1.

   a. How many cupcakes have cherries on top?_____

   b. How many cupcakes do not have cherries on top? _____

2. Circle the row with the most cupcakes.

3. Color the cupcakes on the graph below.

Cupcakes

blue	red	yellow

   a. What is the most popular color?

   _____

   b. What is the least popular color?

   _____

   c. How many cupcakes altogether?

   _____

   d. How many more yellow cupcakes are there than red cupcakes?

   _____

   e. How many more blue cupcakes are there than yellow cupcakes?

   _____

74

© *Teacher Created Resources, Inc.*

Name   **Date**

Molly Muddlemiss was a very fussy eater. This is a graph of the foods she ate in one week.

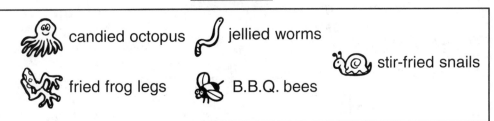

MOLLY'S FOOD

Saturday

Friday

Thursday

Wednesday

Tuesday

Monday

Sunday

1. On what day did she eat the most? _____

2. On what day did she eat the most B.B.Q. bees? _____

3. What food did she really like on Wednesday? _____

4. When do you think she was feeling sick? _____

5. List 3 other foods Molly might like. _____

75

MORE GRAPHS

Unit 2

Interpreting information
Completing graphs
Answering questions
Writing questions
Making a graph

Objectives

- *recognizes and compares the sizes of groups through a variety of estimating, matching, one-to-one correspondence, and counting*
- *counts collections up to 10 objects and beyond*
- *participates in classifying and sequencing objects or pictures*
- *conducts simple data investigation and interprets the results using concrete materials*
- *makes block graphs using one-to-one correspondence between real data and representation*
- *uses appropriate language and representations in describing and interpreting collections of data*
- *describes orally and in writing what displays of data show*
- *compares groups using objects to represent other groups*
- *reads and interprets graphs made from objects*
- *represents addition and subtraction facts up to 20 using concrete materials and in a symbolic way*
- *comments on information in displays produced by himself or herself and others*

Language

how many, graph, block graph, square, key, total, row, column, same, favorite, least, equal

Materials/Resources

counters, plastic cubes, colored pencils

Contents of Student Pages

* *Material needed for each reproducible student page*

Page 78 Counting Data
answering questions, and then coloring squares to complete the graph
* *colored pencils*

Page 79 Interpret Information
Interpret information from a calendar showing the weather and then coloring squares to complete a graph

Page 80 Using Information
Using information from a picture, coloring squares to complete a graph, interpreting the picture to answer questions, writing own questions
* *colored pencils*

Page 81 Interpret a Birthday Graph
Interpreting a graph and adding information to it

Page 82 Interpret an Ice Cream Graph
Interpret a graph and answer questions, drawing groups of objects to match each total
* *colored pencils*

Page 83 Make a Graph
making a graph by coloring in squares using given information and then answering questions
* *colored pencils*

Page 84 Assessment
* *colored pencils*

Remember

Before starting ensure that each student:
- ❑ *has a sharp pencil and colored pencils.*
- ❑ *has an understanding that graphs represent groups of objects.*

76

Additional Activities

❑ *Provide students with lots of opportunities to record information using various materials (e.g., counters, buttons, or blocks) and then to represent the information by making graphs.*

❑ *Integrate graphs with other math strands and other key learning areas (e.g., science—things that float/sink).*

❑ *Record the weather each day for a month with the students. At the end of the month, as a class, make a pictorial graph (later a column graph).*

❑ *Encourage each student to make a graph and exchange it with another student. Each student tells the student who made the graph what information the graph conveys.*

❑ *Encourage students to put graphs in a class book on graphs and/or choose one to be pinned on a notice board each week.*

❑ *Give students practice in making keys and using them in graph making.*

❑ *If some students are having difficulty with the more abstract graphs, give them more experience with comparing groups and representing them pictorially.*

❑ *Provide modeling experiences for the students on reading and interpreting graphs.*

❑ *As a class, collect data and make many simple graphs (e.g., television programs we like, favorite toys, favorite colors, favorite authors). Display graphs and change frequently.*

Answers

Page 78 Counting Data
1. a. 5
   b. 2
   c. 3
   d. 1
2. bus = 2 squares
   truck = 3 squares
   car = 5 squares
   motorcycle = 1 square

Page 79 Interpret Information
1. a. rainy = 10, sunny = 11, windy = 5, cloudy = 5
   b. 1
   c. 5
   d. 10
2. cloudy = 5 squares, sunny = 11 squares, windy = 5 squares, rainy = 10 squares

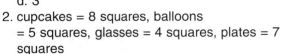

Page 80 Using Information
1. a. 5
   b. 7
   c. 2
   d. 3
2. cupcakes = 8 squares, balloons = 5 squares, glasses = 4 squares, plates = 7 squares
3. a. Answers will vary.
   b. Answers will vary.

Page 81 Interpret a Birthday Graph
1. a. 4
   b. 2
   c. 2
   d. 2
   e. 14
   f. 13
2. Make sure one gray square is added to May and one black square to February.
   a. February, July, September
   b. May, August

Page 82 Interpret an Ice Cream Graph
1. a. red
   b. blue
   c. green, yellow
   d. 3
   e. 7
   f. 12
   g. 29
2. red = 8, green = 5, orange = 7, yellow = 5, blue = 1, pink = 3

Page 83 Make a Graph
1. dog = 13, cat = 8, fish = 3, mouse = 9
2. dog = 13 squares colored, cat = 8 squares colored, fish = 3 squares colored, mouse = 9 squares colored
3. a. 13
   b. 8
   c. fish
   d. fish
   e. 1
   f. Answers will vary.

Page 84 Assessment
Answers based on your class results.

Name	Date

These vehicles were seen passing the school.

1. **a.** How many cars were seen? _____

    b. How many buses were seen? _____

    c. How many trucks were seen? _____

    d. How many motorcycles were seen? _____

2. Color a square for each vehicle seen.

Traffic Survey

#8991 *Targeting Math: Geometry, Chance and Data*

© *Teacher Created Resources, Inc.*

Name	Date

This shows the weather for each day in March.

KEY: = sunny ☂ = rainy ☁ = cloudy ✦ = windy

March

Sunday	Monday	Tuesday	Wednesday	Thursday	Friday	Saturday
	1 ☀	2 ☀	3 ☀	4 ☀	5 ☀	6 ☂
7 ☂	8 ☂	9 ☁	10 ✦	11 ☂	12 ☂	13 ✦
14 ☀	15 ☁	16 ☀	17 ✦	18 ☁	19 ☂	20 ☂
21 ☂	22 ☂	23 ☀	24 ☀	25 ✦	26 ✦	27 ☀
28 ☀	29 ☁	30 ☂	31 ☁			

1. **a.** How many days were:

   rainy? _____

   sunny? _____

   windy? _____

   cloudy? _____

   b. How many more days were sunny than rainy? _____

   c. How many more days were rainy than cloudy? _____

   d. How many days were cloudy or windy? _____

2. Complete this graph using the information shown above.

☁ cloudy													
☀ sunny													
✦ windy													
☂ rainy													

© *Teacher Created Resources, Inc.*   *#8991 Targeting Math: Geometry, Chance and Data*

Name	**Date**

1. **a.** How many balloons? _____

    b. How many plates? _____

    c. How many more plates than balloons? _____

    d. How many more cupcakes than balloons? _____

2. Complete the graph by coloring in squares.

3. **a.** Write a title or name for the graph.

    b. Write a question about the graph.

    _____

    _____

_____ (title)

cupcakes	balloons	glasses	plates

Key ▪ = 1 object

80

Name	Date

The children in second grade made a graph of their birthdays.
The boys are in black and the girls are in gray.

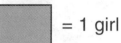

KEY   ■ = 1 boy

       ▨ = 1 girl

Our Birthdays

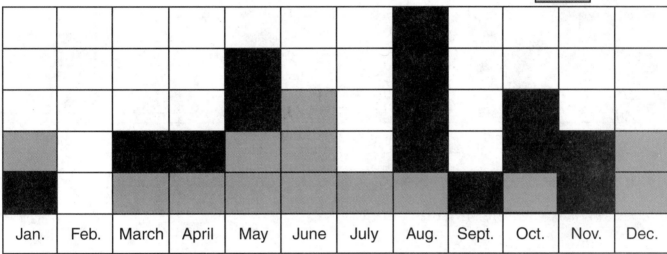

| Jan. | Feb. | March | April | May | June | July | Aug. | Sept. | Oct. | Nov. | Dec. |

1. **a.** How many have birthdays in May? _____

   b. How many have birthdays in December? _____

   c. How many months have 3 birthdays in them? _____

   d. The month of March has _____ more birthdays than February.

   e. How many boys are there? _____

   f. How many girls are there? _____

2. In June, Maria and Peter joined second grade. Maria's birthday is in May and Peter's is in February. Add them to the graph. Answer the questions.

   a. Which three months have the least number of birthdays?

   _____ , _____ , and _____

   b. Which two months have the most birthdays?

   _____ and _____

⁸¹

Name	Date

Favorite Color of Ice Cream of the Second Grade Class

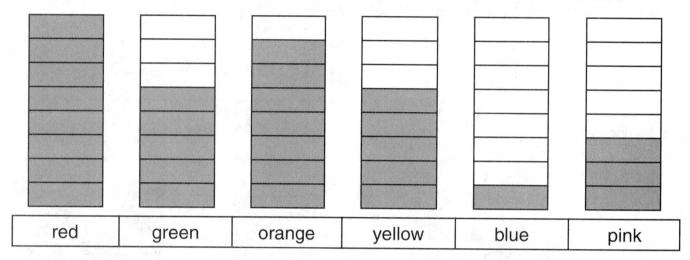

red	green	orange	yellow	blue	pink

1. Look at the graph of favorite color of ice cream. ▢ = 1 child

   a. Which was the most favorite color?   _____

   b. Which was the least favorite color?   _____

   c. Which colors scored the same?   _____ and _____

   d. How many children liked pink?   _____

   e. How many children liked orange?   _____

   f. How many children altogether liked green and orange ice cream?   _____

   g. How many children are in the second grade class?   _____

2. Carefully count each column. Draw an ice cream on the graph for each person in the space below. The first color is done for you. Then color the ice cream.

    red   green   orange

⑧②   yellow   blue   pink

Name	**Date**

1. The class collected the following information using counters. Count the total for each category.

Favorite Animals

dog	cat	fish	mouse
○ ○ ○ ○ ○	○ ○ ○	○ ○ ○	○ ○ ○ ○
○ ○ ○ ○ ○	○ ○ ○ ○		○ ○ ○ ○
○ ○ ○	○		○

Total: _____   Total: _____   Total: _____   Total: _____

2. Make your own graph from the information. Color one square for each person.

3. Answer these questions.

    a. How many children like dogs? _____

    b. How many children like cats? _____

    c. What is the least popular animal? _____

    d. Cats are more popular than _____ .

    e. How many more children prefer mice than cats? _____

    f. What other animals could there have been?

© *Teacher Created Resources, Inc.*   *#8991 Targeting Math: Geometry, Chance and Data*

Name	**Date**

Make a graph of hair colors in your class.

1. Count the students using counters or plastic cubes.

2. Write your totals in the boxes below.

blonde = ☐   black = ☐   brown = ☐   red = ☐

blonde   black   brown   red

3. Color in each column to show the totals.

4. Write the title for the graph on the line under the graph.

5. Write 3 questions for your graph.

a. _____

_____

_____

_____

b. _____

_____

_____

_____

c. _____

_____

_____

_____

84 _____
(title)

CHANCE AND DATA

The concepts of will, won't, might happen, certain/
uncertain, possible/impossible, and likely/unlikely are
all contained in this unit on chance and data. Students
must decide on the chances of an event occurring. They
collect, interpret, and graph data. They use tally marks
to record the times an event occurs and summarize the
results. Interviewing classmates is a fun way of learning
to organize data that has to be presented. The activity
page is a game where a correct prediction is a decided
help to being the winner. There is one assessment page
in each unit.

© Teacher Created Resources, Inc.

BEGINNING CHANCE AND DATA

Unit 1

Understanding chance
Collecting data
Classifying
Ordering
Summarizing

Objectives

- uses language associated with uncertainty
- shows some recognition of the element of chance in familiar daily activities
- with guidance, poses questions about collected objects and information
- classifies objects using one or two familiar criteria
- places objects into sequences using familiar criteria
- displays objects and pictures and describes data in words and numbers
- represents objects or people in pictorial displays to record the results of data collection
- uses displays to make simple comparisons
- summarizes information by counting

Language

chance, chances, collecting, common, could, couldn't, data, happen, how many, like, less, many, might, more, most, order, popular, same, sort, will, won't, which, least

Materials/Resources

writing/drawing materials, fruits, lunch boxes, colored pencils, glue, scissors, dice, counters

Contents of Student Pages

* Materials needed for each reproducible student page

Page 88 Chance Language
understanding chance language—will, won't, and might
* drawing materials

Page 89 More Chance Language
understanding chance language—won't, will, and might happen
* drawing materials

Page 90 Collecting Data
drawing fruit found in friends' lunch boxes; counting fruit; interpreting data
* fruit in students' lunchboxes, colored pencils

Page 91 Classifying
classifying similar things, sorting into groups, ordering
* colored pencils, scissors, glue

Page 92 Weather
observing and drawing weather, interpreting results
* colored pencils

Page 93 Coming to School
interviewing, recording, interpreting, and summarizing data
* colored pencils

Page 94 Assessment
* drawing materials

Page 95 Activity—Predictions
* 1 die, different colored counters for each player

Remember

❑ Relate classroom activities to chance and data whenever possible.

❑ Use a variety of vocabulary when discussing chance and data.

❑ Make students aware that chance events do not happen definitely.

❑ Use data that is easily obtainable for students.

© Teacher Created Resources, Inc.

Additional Activities

❑ *Obtain data from various sources—television, peers, teacher, parents, books, films, traffic, etc. Collate and interpret.*

❑ *Investigate all the places where chance events occur (e.g., races, Lotto, or games).*

❑ *Try to predict the weather each day and see if predictions were correct. Graph the results and interpret the data.*

❑ *Discuss, draw, and write about different things. Which ones will, won't, might, could, and couldn't happen at different ages, times of the year, in different places, etc.?*

Answers

Page 88 Chance Language
Teacher to check.

Page 89 More Chance Language
1. Circle pictures of sleeping and flying in a balloon.
2. Circle pictures of reading a book and working at a desk.
3. Teacher to check.

Page 90 Collecting Data
Teacher to check.

Page 91 Classifying
1. leaves, trees, house, and/or pencil (made of wood)
2. 2, 3, 1, 4
3. Fruit: bananas, apple, grapes
   Transportation: car, plane, bus, bicycle

Page 92 Weather
Teacher to check.

Page 93 Coming to School
Teacher to check.

Page 94 Assessment
1. Teacher to check.
2. Teacher to check.
3. all wood
4. a. 8
   b. 5
   c. heart
   d. circle
   e. Favorite Shapes

Page 95 Activity—Predictions
Teacher to check.

Name	**Date**

1. Draw something you *will* do this afternoon.

2. Draw something you *won't* do this afternoon.

3. Draw something you *might* do this afternoon.

     © *Teacher Created Resources, Inc.*

Name	**Date**

1. Color the things that *won't happen* at lunch.

2. Color the things that *will happen* today.

3. Draw two things that *might happen* today.

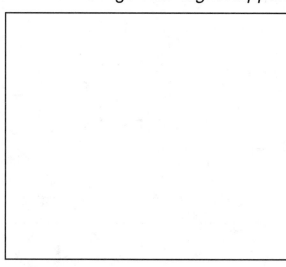

89

Name	**Date**

1. Draw the fruits in your friends' lunch boxes.

2. How many are there of each fruit?

apples   🍎   ☐   bananas   🍌   ☐

oranges   🍊   ☐   pears   🍐   ☐

grapes   🍇   ☐   other types   ☐

3. Which fruit is most common? _____

4. What is your favorite fruit? _____

90

Name	**Date**

1. Color the things that are *like* each other.

2. Label these in *order* from smallest to largest.

 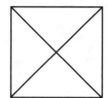 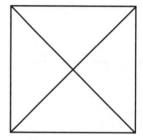

_____   _____   _____   _____

3. Cut out the items below and sort them into two groups. Glue them into the right group.

Group 1	Group 2

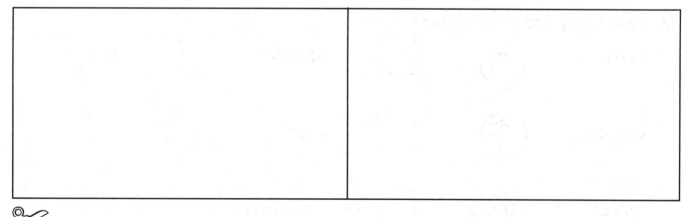

91

Name	Date

1. Look at the weather for one school week. Draw pictures of it.

Monday	Tuesday	Wednesday	Thursday	Friday

2. How many:

   a. sunny days? _____

   b. rainy days? _____

   c. cloudy days? _____

3. Which days were:

   a. sunny? _____

   b. rainy? _____

Name	**Date**

1. Ask 10 people in your class how they come to school.

2. Color what you found.

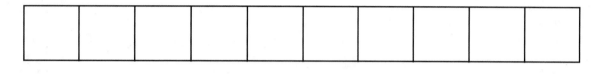

= 1 person

car

bus

walk

other

3. How many came by:

   a. car? _____   **b.** bus? _____

   c. walking? _____   **d.** other? _____

4. Complete.

   a. Most children came by _____ .

   b. More children came by _____ than by _____ .

© *Teacher Created Resources, Inc.*

Name	**Date**

1. Draw something that *will* and *won't* happen tonight.

Will	**Won't**

2. What *might* happen tomorrow? _____

_____

3. How are these things the same?

     _____

_____

4. Look at the graph and answer the questions.

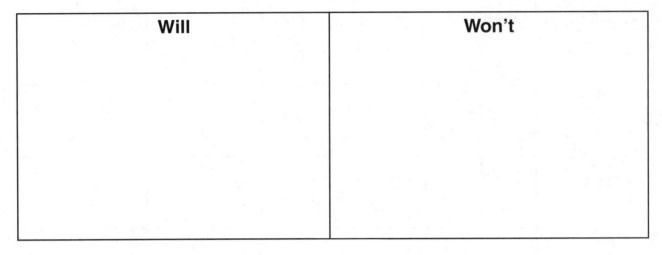

   a. How many: hearts? _____   **b.** squares? _____

   c. The most popular shape is _____ .

   d. The least popular shape is _____ .

   e. Write a good title or name for the graph. _____

94

Name　　　　　　　　　　　　　　　　　　**Date**

Materials: 1 die and a different colored counter for each player
Number of players: 4
How to play:
- Players take turns rolling the die.
- Before rolling, the player must predict the result. If the prediction is correct, double the number and move that number of squares. If the prediction is wrong, move only the number shown on the die.
- If you land on a sad face, move backward on your next turn.
- If you land on a smiley face, have another turn.
- The first person to the star is the winner.

64 ☆	63	62 ☹	61	60	59	58 ☹	57
49	50	51	52 ☺	53	54	55	56
48	47	46 ☺	45	44 ☹	43	42	41
33 ☺	34	35	36	37	38 ☺	39	40 ☹
32	31	30 ☹	29	28	27	26	25
17 ☹	18	19	20	21	22 ☺	23	24
16	15	14	13	12	11 ☹	10	9
1	2	3 ☺	4	5	6	7	8

START

© Teacher Created Resources, Inc.

MORE CHANCE AND DATA

Unit 2

Possible
Impossible
Predictions
Collecting data
Graphs

Objectives

- distinguishes impossible from unlikely events
- distinguishes impossible from possible events, and describes familiar and easily understood events as more likely or less likely to happen
- shows some recognition of the element of chance in familiar daily activities
- recognizes that different results are possible when some actions are repeated
- collects data in the form of information to answer his or her questions
- contributes to deciding how to classify and sequence data, applying unambiguous and familiar criteria consistently
- displays and summarizes data based on one-to-one correspondence between data and representation
- describes how a graph shows the results of data collection
- writes brief descriptions of data collection

Language

altogether, data, dice, die, exactly, favorite, fewer, graph, groups, guess, happen, head, how many, impossible, interview, least, less, likely, more, most, popular, next, number, possible, possibly, probability, result, roll, same, second most, tail, tallies, throw, toss, type, unlikely

Materials/Resources

writing/drawing materials, dice, coins

Contents of Student Pages
  * Materials needed for each reproducible student page

Page 98 Possible and Impossible
likelihood of events happening—possible and impossible events, matching events to labels
  * colored pencils

Page 99 What's the Chance?
rolling a die, interpreting and predicting results
  * dice

Page 100 Collecting Data
collecting and interpreting data, making statements

Page 101 Organizing Data
tossing a coin to collect data, interpreting results, grouping data
  * coins

Page 102 Presenting Data
graphing and interpreting data
  * colored pencils

Page 103 Favorite Songs
graphing favorite songs and interpreting data
  * colored pencils

Page 104 Assessment
  * colored pencils, dice

Remember

- ❏ Relate classroom activities to chance and data whenever possible.
- ❏ Tell students that bar and column graphs start from zero on the left hand side.
- ❏ Use a variety of vocabulary when discussing chance and data.

© Teacher Created Resources, Inc.

Additional Activities

❏ *Discuss different kinds of graphs—bar, pie, column, line, and picture.*

❏ *Play games involving chance.*

❏ *Look for places in the environment (e.g., on television, in newspapers, etc.) where graphs are used.*

❏ *Obtain data from various sources such as television, peers, teachers, parents, books, films, or traffic. Collate and interpret.*

❏ *Watch sporting events and try to predict numbers. Discuss the difficulty of doing so.*

❏ *Find a paragraph in the newspaper. Estimate the chance of finding certain words in that passage. Read the paragraph to see if estimates were correct. Discuss chance and the probability of these being correct.*

Answers

Page 98 Possible and Impossible
Teacher to check.

Page 99 What's the Chance?
Teacher to check.

Page 100 Collecting Data
Teacher to check.

Page 101 Organizing Data
Teacher to check.

Page 102 Presenting Data
1. a.

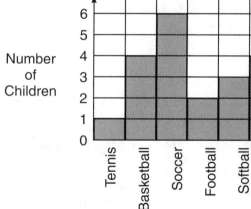

    b. soccer
    c. 20
2. Teacher to check.

Page 103 Favorite Songs
Teacher to check.

Page 104 Assessment
1. Teacher to check.
2. No, too unpredictable
3.

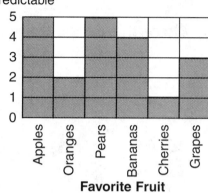

a. 5
b. 20
c. Teacher to check.

Name	**Date**

1. Color the things that could *possibly* happen today.

2. Draw two things that are *impossible*.

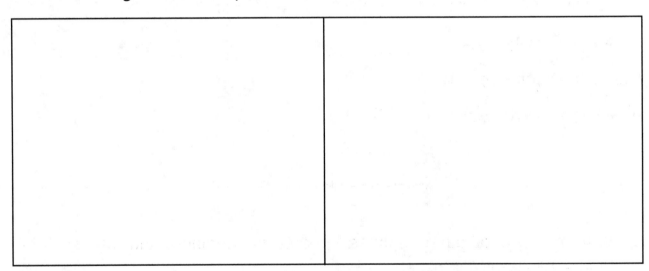

3. Match each of these events to the word *likely, possibly, unlikely,* or *impossible*.

have dinner	**LIKELY**	meet your favorite star
visit grandparents	**POSSIBLE**	snow at school
go shopping	**UNLIKELY**	get 100% in a test
	IMPOSSIBLE	

98

| Name | Date |

1. **a.** Roll a die 4 times. Write down what you rolled.

   Roll 1: _____ Roll 2: _____

   Roll 3: _____ Roll 4: _____

   b. Did you always get the same number? _____

   c. Which number did you roll 3 times? _____

   d. Which number did you roll 2 times? _____

   e. Which number do you think you will roll next? _____

   f. Try it and see. Answer: _____ Were you right? _____

2. **a.** Can you always guess the number? _____

   b. Why or why not? _____

   _____

3. With a friend, roll a die 10 times. Record the numbers and discuss what happened.

   a. _____ **b.** _____ **c.** _____

   d. _____ **e.** _____ **f.** _____

   g. _____ **h.** _____ **i.** _____

   j. _____

99

Name	Date

1. Ask your classmates which of these TV shows they like best. Use tally marks to record the results.

TV Show	Tally Marks	Total
Cartoons		
Music Shows		
Sports		
Other		

2. **a.** How many like cartoons? _____

  b. How many like music shows? _____

  c. How many like other kinds of TV shows? _____

  d. How many like sports? _____

  e. Which TV show was the most popular? _____

3. Complete.

  a. There were more votes for _____ than for _____ .

  b. There were fewer votes for _____ than for _____ .

  c. The least popular show was _____ .

100

Name	**Date**

1. **a.** Toss a coin 12 times and record heads or tails.

＿＿＿＿　　＿＿＿＿　　＿＿＿＿　　＿＿＿＿　　＿＿＿＿　　＿＿＿＿
　1　　　　　2　　　　　3　　　　　4　　　　　5　　　　　6

＿＿＿＿　　＿＿＿＿　　＿＿＿＿　　＿＿＿＿　　＿＿＿＿　　＿＿＿＿
　7　　　　　8　　　　　9　　　　　10　　　　11　　　　12

b. How many times did you toss:

a head? ＿＿＿＿＿　　　　　　　　a tail? ＿＿＿＿＿

c. Would the results be exactly the same if you tossed the coin another 12 times? ＿＿＿＿＿＿＿＿

d. Try it. What happened? ＿＿＿＿＿＿＿＿＿＿＿＿＿＿＿＿＿＿＿＿

2. If you had to do a project on 5 animals in your neighborhood, how would you group them? Write them in the boxes.

3. **a.** If you had to find out what your classmates had for lunch, what 8 groups would you make? Write them in the boxes.

b. Did everyone in the class make the same groups? ＿＿＿＿＿＿＿＿＿

(101)

Name	**Date**

1. Some children were asked their favorite sport. These are the results.

   Tennis—1   Basketball—4   Soccer—6

   Football—2   Softball—3   Baseball—4

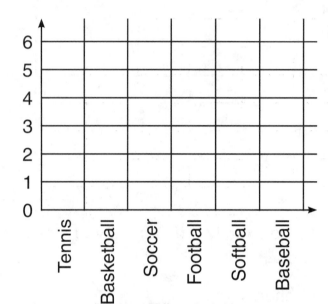

   a. Color the graph to show the children's favorite sports.

   b. Which is the most popular sport? _____

   c. How many children are there altogether? _____

2. Ask your class what their favorite toy is and fill in the graph with your results.

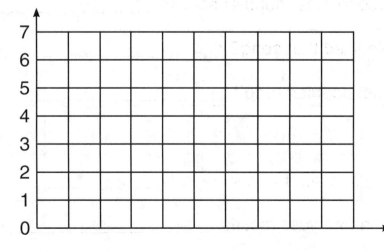

#8991 Targeting Math: Geometry, Chance and Data   © *Teacher Created Resources, Inc.*

Name	**Date**

1. Ask your classmates what their favorite song is and graph your results.

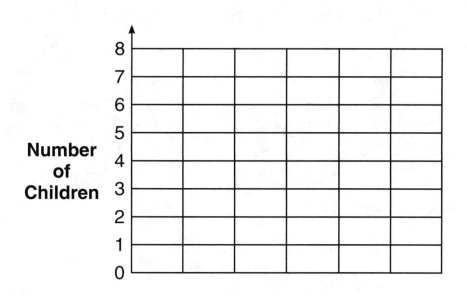

Favorite Song

2. What was the most popular song? _____

3. How many people liked that song? _____

4. What was the second most popular song? _____

5. How many people liked that song? _____

6. What was the least popular song? _____

7. How many people did you interview? _____

8. What would be a good title for this graph? _____

9. Write a sentence about your results. _____

Name	**Date**

1. Color red the things that *possibly* will happen today.

   Color blue the things that *will not* happen today. (They are impossible.)

2. Using one die, is it easy to roll a 6? _____

   Why?_____

3. Graph the favorite fruit of some children.

   Apples—5   Oranges—2   Pears—5

   Bananas—4   Cherries—1   Grapes—3

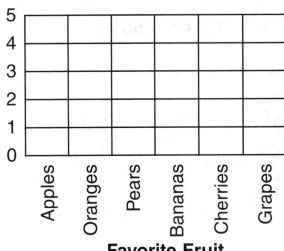

   Favorite Fruit

   a. How many liked oranges and grapes? _____

   b. How many children were there altogether? _____

   c. Write two sentences about the results.

   _____

   _____

#8991 Targeting Math: Geometry, Chance and Data   © *Teacher Created Resources, Inc.*

Name	**Date**

© *Teacher Created Resources, Inc.*

Name	**Date**

#8991 *Targeting Math: Geometry, Chance and Data*

© *Teacher Created Resources, Inc.*

Name	**Date**

© *Teacher Created Resources, Inc.*

Name	**Date**

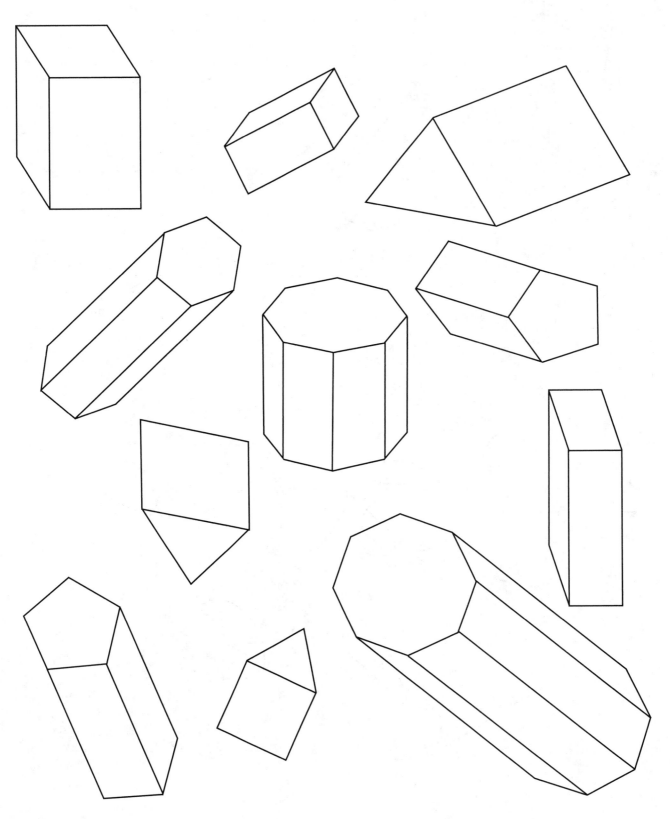

© Teacher Created Resources, Inc.

Name   **Date**

© *Teacher Created Resources, Inc.*   *#8991 Targeting Math: Geometry, Chance and Data*

Name   **Date**

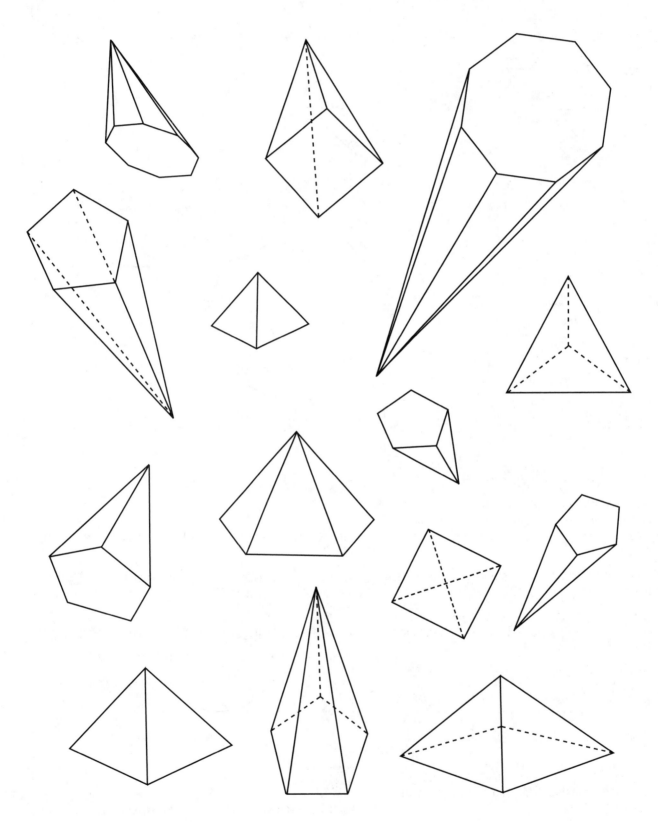

Skills Index

The following index lists specific objectives for the student pages of each unit in the book. The objectives are grouped according to the sections listed in the Table of Contents. Use the Skills Index as a resource for identifying the units and student pages you wish to use.

Two-Dimensional Shapes

generally recognizes and names triangles, rectangles, circles and common simple shapes (Pages: 11, 19)

interprets and begins to use terms relating to shape to distinguish similarities and differences (Page: 11)

makes two-dimensional shapes using geo-boards (Page: 18)

makes, classifies, and names two-dimensional shapes and describes their properties (Page: 18)

makes constructions from verbal and visual instructions (Page: 23)

matches congruent figures and objects one to one (Page: 19)

names mathematical shapes, which can be found as components of familiar things (Page: 13)

recognizes, describes, and makes and continues simple number and spatial patterns (Page: 20)

recognizes, names, and makes simple two-dimensional shapes and describes their properties using everyday language by observing similarities and differences (Pages: 10, 12, 22)

sorts and describes objects in terms of their features such as size and shape (Pages: 8, 9, 13)

talks about likenesses and differences between things seen or handled and begins to connect shape to function (Page: 21)

Three-Dimensional Shapes

classifies objects by a familiar attribute relating to shape (Page: 29)

counts collections up to 10 objects and beyond (Page: 32)

describes three-dimensional objects using everyday language, models and sorts them, and recognizes them in drawings (Pages: 31, 32)

distinguishes between a three-dimensional object and its face (Page: 33)

explores and describes faces, edges, and corners of three-dimensional objects (Pages: 30, 33, 40)

investigates and describes objects from different points of view (Page: 41)

makes stacking and packing patterns of three-dimensional objects that will stack or pack (Page: 43)

names mathematical shapes which can be found as components of familiar things (Page: 38)

sorts and describes objects in terms of their features such as size and shape (Pages: 28, 39)

Position and Mapping/Transformation

describes the location of an object in relation to other objects (Page: 51)

finds paths on simple maps and mazes (Page: 53)

generates patterns and follows rules based on the simple repetition and movement of things (Pages: 61, 63)

makes a decorative pattern (Page: 58)

makes symmetrical patterns (Page: 59)

repeats, orients, and turns over things when making patterns (Page: 62)

represents the position of objects using pictures, sketches, and models and uses everyday language to describe their position (Pages: 50, 51, 52)

uses everyday language associated with position (Page: 48)

uses and understands the language of movement (Page: 60)

uses and understands the language of position (Page: 49)

Graphs

comments on information in displays produced by himself or herself and others (Page: 81)

compares groups using objects to represent other groups (Pages: 72, 73, 80)

compares groups using pictorial representations (Page: 70)

111

Skills Index

conducts simple data investigation and interprets the results using concrete materials (Pages: 79, 83)

counts collections up to 10 objects and beyond (Pages: 68, 70, 71, 72, 78, 82)

describes orally and in writing what displays of data show (Page: 80)

displays objects and pictures and describes data in words and numbers (Page: 73)

displays and summarizes data based on one-to-one correspondence between data and representation (Page: 71)

makes block graphs using one-to-one correspondence between real data and representation (Pages: 79, 83)

makes simple pictographs using one-to-one correspondence between real data and a representation (Page: 69)

participates in classifying and sequencing objects or pictures (Pages: 69, 78)

reads and interprets graphs made from objects (Pages: 81, 82)

recognizes and compares the sizes of groups through a variety of strategies such as estimating, matching, one-to-one correspondence, and counting (Pages: 68, 78, 82)

represents addition and subtraction facts up to 20 using concrete materials and in a symbolic way (Page: 81)

selects and carries out the operation appropriate to situations involving addition and subtraction (Pages: 70, 72, 73)

sorts and describes in terms of their features such as size and shape (Page 69)

uses appropriate language and representations in describing and interpreting collections of data (Page: 80)

Chance and Data

classifies objects using one or two familiar criteria (Page: 91)

collects data in the form of information to answer his or her questions (Page: 100)

contributes to deciding how to classify and sequence data, applying unambiguous and familiar criteria consistently (Page: 101)

describes how a graph shows the results of data collection (Page: 103)

displays objects and pictures and describes data in words and numbers (Page: 92)

displays and summarizes data based on one-to-one correspondence between data and representation (Page: 102)

distinguishes impossible from possible events, and describes familiar and easily understood events as more likely or less likely to happen (Page: 98)

distinguishes impossible from unlikely events (Page: 98)

places objects into sequences using familiar criteria (Page: 91)

recognizes that different results are possible when some actions are repeated (Page: 99)

represents objects or people in pictorial displays to record the results of data collection (Pages: 92, 93)

shows some recognition of the element of chance in familiar daily activities (Pages: 88, 99)

summarizes information by counting (Page: 93)

uses displays to make simple comparisons (Page: 93)

uses language associated with uncertainty (Pages: 88, 89)

with guidance, poses questions about collected objects and information (Page: 90)

writes brief descriptions of data collection (Page: 103)

#8991 Targeting Math: Geometry, Chance and Data

© Teacher Created Resources, Inc.